MALABAR AND ITS FOLK

MALABAR AND ITS FOLK

BY

T. K. GOPAL PANIKKAR, B.A.

WITH AN INTRODUCTION

BY THE

REV. F. W. KELLETT, M.A.

(of the Madras Christian College.)

GYAN

Published by

GYAN

Gyan Publishing House
5, Ansari Road
Daryaganj, New Delhi-110002
Phone: 011-47034999, 9811692060
E-mail: books@gyanbooks.com

Distribution Network
gyanbooks.com
India, USA, Canada, UK, Australia, France

ISBN : 978-81-212-4534-0 (HB)
First Published, 1900

2nd Impression 2020

Printed at: Gyan Press, Delhi.

The book at your disposal is the edition of an old book originally published long back. The Text quality of this book may not be at par as compared to our other books but many readers approached us to reprint this important book so that it could satiate their hunger. We request all the readers of this book to help us to improve its quality by providing the necessary text of those pages which are not properly visible. Your valuable support in this case will be highly appreciated and acknowledged and our future readers will be benefitted immensely.

Malabar and its Folk

BY

T. K. GOPAL PANIKKAR, B.A.

WITH AN INTRODUCTION

BY THE

REV. F. W. KELLETT, M. A.
(of the Madras Christian College.)

Madras:

G. A. NATESAN & CO., PRINTERS, ESPLANADE ROW.

1900.

DEDICATED

BY KIND PERMISSION

TO

Mr. G. W. Dance, I.C.S.

(Collector of Malabar.)

CONTENTS.

INTRODUCTION

WHEN Mr. Gopal Panikkar pressed me as his old teacher to write a few sentences by way of introduction to this book, I felt that, though one who could lend a better known name would have been a more influential sponsor to it, I could not refuse his repeated request. And indeed it gives me no little pleasure to trace in these pages the germination of the interest implanted in him by our study in the Madras Christian College of the rudiments of Ethnography and the history of Early Institutions.

And here lies one of the elements of general interest which the book possesses. What is the effect of Western studies on Hindu minds? To this common question the book affords an answer. The reader will see plainly here the manner in which, and the extent to which, Indian gentlemen of education are assimilating the science of the West and in its light modifying their views of Indian life and tradition.

This leads on to another element of value possessed by the book. Graduates of Indian Universities may legitimately be expected to transmit to those of their fellow countrymen who have not had their advantages the illumination from the West which they have themselves received. It is through them above all that what is good in Western civilisation and thought must reach the Indian mind. More of them are discharging this duty than is sometimes supposed. Mr. Gopal Panikkar's book is well adapted to open up lines along which new modes of thought may pass to the minds of thinking men in Malabar and from them to the people in general. Never perhaps have the national customs and beliefs of an Indian district been set forth in fresh light so freely by a native of that district as in this book. Mr. Gopal Panikkar has not lost his affection for the customs of Malabar, any more than the ethnographer of the West has lost his love for May-day customs because he sees in them survivals of obsolete modes of life; but he sees them from a higher point of view and with a truer and more comprehensive vision than the mass of his neighbours. And so his book should have for them the value of interpreting to them some of the practices whose meaning they have wholly or partially lost.

But the book appeals to a wider circle. In these days when ethnography and primitive habits and folklore have awakened so general an interest, chapters like these have a value which will be at once recognized. Even if Malabar were a region that possessed no special claims on the attention of students of sociology an account of it by a native would be welcome. Most ethnographic descriptions even of Indian districts have been written by European observers and bear the traces of the European mind. In this book we have a native of the country, familiar with its customs from his earliest days, setting forth its social, legal and religious life. I believe that this is the first book of the kind of which this can be said, a distinction which gives it a special claim to notice. Defects no doubt are conspicuous enough, but in a pioneer such are readily forgiven.

But Malabar is no ordinary Indian district. Both district and people are clearly marked off from the rest of India and have features all their own. As even a glance at the contents of this book will show, they have a social organisation, marriage customs, a law of inheritance, festivals and religious rites that distinguish them from their neighbours. Mr. Gopal Panikkar frequently mentions what he regards as parallels in nations of other times and places, and though the parallels may not be always as complete as he supposes, there is deep interest in such comparative study. Apart from those comparisons which he draws, a hundred others will suggest themselves to the student of society, ritual and folk-lore. Similarity and dissimilarity alike will stimulate thought. India, as Sir Henry Maine said, is an assemblage of fragments of ancient society; but perhaps no part of India contains fragments of such variety and importance as Malabar. To many the name will suggest the one strange custom of Nair Polyandry, a custom now rapidly disappearing. This book will show them many others no less interesting. Maine called for immediate study of these archaic fragments, because the spread of Western civilisation was sweeping them away. To the rapidity with which this process is going on this book bears witness. Mr. Gopal Panikkar has deserved well of sociologists in setting down in black and white a description of Malabar customs before that process has gone any further.

F. W. KELLETT.

PREFACE.

MY object in placing this book before the public is to present in a brief compass some of the salient phases of social and religious life in Malabar. The major portion of the book, it will be observed, deals with the life and institutions of the Nairs, by far the most conspicuous amongst the peoples of Malabar. The book is a first attempt of the kind at a systematic treatment of the subject. It is far from being an exhaustive treatise. I do not claim any universality of application so far as the entire district is concerned for the customs and institutions described in the book; but, at all events, I wish to point out that the descriptions given will be found to apply to some part, more particularly the South, if not the whole of Malabar. The social customs and institutions of Malabar are so varied and conflicting that it would be fruitless to attempt to give an accurate and exhaustive account of them. Those that obtain in one village may be, and in fact sometimes are, essentially distinct in detail from those that obtain in the village or villages adjoining it. In some places certain peculiar customs prevail which are entirely absent in others. In North Malabar the state of things is essentially different, and the Northerners do not cherish certain customs and institutions which find favor with their brethren of the South. In ways such as these our social and domestic life presents diversities in detail.

The social frame like the human body is constantly undergoing changes by slow and imperceptible gradations; the nature of these changes being more or less dependent upon the kind of food with which that body is nourished. We are being fed on the strong food of Western science and civilisation; and it is no wonder that our life and society are passing through changes resulting from living contact with the West. In the interests of the science of sociology it is extremely necessary to preserve a permanent record of those Indian customs and institutions which are rapidly decaying.

The various chapters of the book except XI and XIV have already appeared in some one or other of the leading Indian Magazines and Journals such as *The Calcutta Review, The Christian College Magazine, The Indian Review, The Pioneer, The Madras Times, The Madras Standard, The Hindu, The Malabar Times and the West Coast Spectator*. I take this opportunity of expressing my gratitude to the editors of these papers for kindly permitting me to reprint them.

I have added a small glossary of vernacular or native terms with which the majority of my readers may be unfamiliar.

I sincerely thank my revered Professor the Rev. F. W. Kellett, M.A. of the Madras Christian College, to whom I am deeply indebted for the kind introduction. My heartfelt thanks are also due to G. W. Dance, Esq., I.C.S., the head of our district for readily allowing me to dedicate this little volume to him.

I hope to bring out in the not distant future, time and circumstances permitting, a companion volume in which I propose to deal more with the antiquities of Malabar than I have been able to do here.

CHOWGHAUT,
8th October 1900.

T. K. GOPAL PANIKKAR.

CHAPTER I.

THOUGHTS ON MALABAR.

MALABAR is an exceedingly interesting district which combines the charms of a hoary antiquity, the beauties of a pleasing scenery and the delightful simplicity of domestic life. It extends from Gokarnam to Cape Comorin from north to south; and its western border is beaten by the waves of the Arabian Sea, while its east is bounded by the districts of Coimbatore, Coorg and part of Mysore. Tradition ascribes its creation to Parasu Rama, one of the incarnations of Vishnu. As recorded in the old Puranas, Parasu Rama, having destroyed the Kshatriya race twenty-one times thought of expiating his sin by making a grant of land to the twice-born Brahmins. With this object in view he prayed to Varuna, the Neptune of our classical Mythology, to create some land for the purpose. The request was granted and the sea-god commanded the Arabian Sea, which then stretched far up to the Ghauts, to recede. The element obeyed his divine mandate and receded as far away as its modern boundaries leaving dry the strip of country now known as Malabar; and this he granted to the Brahmins in expiation for his sin; and ever since Malabar has been a Brahmin country dominated by a Brahmin aristocracy. To this day the Brahmin power is practically unchecked in the Native States of Cochin and Travancore.

Another version of the story makes the creation of Malabar the sole work of Parasu Rama himself. He assumed his full divine powers and the sea had to submit to his orders. He took a sieve, and forcefully threw it along the surface of the waters. With the forward career of the sieve, the sea also receded; and the recession stopped only when the sieve came to a standstill. In this way by many repetitions of the process of throwing the sieve Parasu Rama reclaimed the whole extent of the land of Malabar.

These traditions, incredible as they seem, may, nevertheless, contain in them a nucleus of true history. It is now admitted by most antiquarians that the Arabian Sea once extended as far inland as the range of mountains now known as 'Kalladikodan.' Natural and geological changes took place in after-times which resulted in a recession of the sea, leaving dry the tract of country identified with Malabar. In course of time, Parasu Rama, a Brahmin from the east, crossed over to the west side of the Ghauts with a train of Brahmin followers whom he settled in the country. The fact that the sea once extended to the Kalladikodan mountains is indicated by the history of the word 'Kalladikodan,' itself which is said to be a corruption of 'Kadaladikodan,' the 'surf-beaten' or 'sea-beaten,' (the change of *d* into *l* being an established rule of philology). This presumption is also evidenced by the fact that shells and bones of exclusively marine animals have been picked up on these mountains from time to time. This is the rationalistic view of the question.

Such, in brief, is the traditional account of the origin of Malabar. The country is interesting from a variety of points of view. Its people, its customs and manners, its institutions, its architecture and its traditions are all so quaintly pristine and so deeply interesting that it affords points of peculiar attraction to the student of Ethnology. Its known history dates, it is said, from the times of St. Thomas, the Apostle. Tradition has it that the Apostle during his evangelistic mission to China and the Eastern countries travelled through Malabar, founding in various places seven churches, remnants of which still survive to bear witness to the possible genuineness of the tradition. It is, at present, no doubt, only a tradition which may or may not contain germs of true history. But, at any rate, there is the tradition and the point is interesting in that it still remains one of the hopeless mysteries of antiquity. Malabar has also the envied fame of being the first place in India ever trod by the venturous foot of the mighty European. The Portuguese and the Dutch first set their foot upon our native soil and have left behind them architectural and monumental impresses which help to impart an element of truth and of history to their quondam manœuvres in it. The great historian of India, Orme, drew his first and last breath from its invigorating atmosphere and his honored dust now remains mixed up with its antique soil. Later and quite recently the forceful career of Tippu striking terror through the length and breadth of the land is still cherished in awful remembrance by the people as if it were a thing of a short yesterday. The numerous Mahomedans now forming part of our native population and the disturbing element in its political history are mostly the living monuments of the times when the religious purity and simplicity of the Hindu household have been forced, at the inexorable point of the sword, to yield to the barefaced corruption and effeminate luxuries of the Mahommedan harem. These are but a few of the points which mark it out as a favourite subject of study and investigation for the historian.

Malabar presents striking analogies to Scotland on the one hand and to Ireland on the other, not in the degree of civilization attained by its people, not in the deep-seated elements of culture and spirit of progressive enlightenment, nor in the stern hardihood and the persevering industry of its people, but in the fascinating charms of its native scenery, in its systematized clan-organization, and in the primitive religious conceptions of its people embodied in ridiculously superstitious tales about fairies, witches, and demons in the one case, and in the other, the politics and the stirring political history marred constantly by the repetition of tales of bloodshed and uprisings on the part of a people groaning under the oppressive yoke of an agrarian despotism and in their blind submission to the mandates of a privileged class.

The Scottish scenery has, for long, impressed deep its magic influence upon the foreign visitor to it or even the readers of its descriptive accounts. Scotland's numerous fells and dales decked with verdant plants and blooming flowers have from time to time, been sung of in immortal verse by poets and written about in deathless characters by novelists. It was not without stirrings of genuine poetic sympathies that "Aristo of the North" enchanted by her mystic influence and caught within her magic fold reverenced and adored her as a

> " Meet nurse for a poetic child
> Land of brown heath and shaggy wood
> Land of the mountain and the flood."

Her natural features have always excited feelings of inspiration in the breasts of all poets and patriots. The even song of the traveller within is ever responsive to the deep and solemn murmur of her gliding rills which form a silvery streak about her rock-built bases. Her stern and wild woodlands rent asunder by craggy, slant or headlong pathways and steps leading through their flowery borders to the ruffled surface of her rippling streams have always afforded the greatest charm even to the least poetic minds. And hills over hills set in gay theatric pride have never failed to captivate the imagination of poets and to present unto them a delightful scenery the like of which is extremely rare. The pearly waters of her Lochs and Creeks, rippling about their rocky bases and lapping on the mossy crags, now girgling through rents and holes constitute another element of interest that centres round the Scottish scenery.

Such, in brief, is the aspect in which Nature presents herself to the visitor amongst the hills and streams of Scotland. Nor is the constitution of her clans and tribes less interesting and instructive. Her clan-organization in which the memories of all the departed souls are kept alive by sacred traditions which have about them the charm of simplicity, has afforded food for observation to the student of Ethnology. Tales of fairies and devils and nymphs which are current amongst the untutored classes have been sung of by her native poets, who wrote about the goblin page escaping from the clutches of one deity by crossing over little parting streams where ended its territorial jurisdiction for mischief-working. The nereids of Scotland's story and the witches of her national tales are both primitive and interesting and have been frequently celebrated in verse by her native poets.

This is but a brief description of the stern and wild Caledonia loved by philosophers and celebrated by poets in rhymes which stand as the glory of British literature. These have likewise their counterparts in our ancient land of Malabar. She also presents fascination to the curious visitor amongst her mountains and rivers. Except on the borders of the sea the major portion of the country is intersected by chains of hills and ranges of mountains, and spanned by streams and streamlets, rivers and rivulets, at intervals overlaid with fields of luxuriant verdure. The traveller in the eastern parts where the sandy tracts are replaced by reddened soil is lost in amazement amidst the loveliness of a scenery unrivalled elsewhere. Fields laden with heavy corn waving yellow in the tepid breeze in which the busy day-labourer basking in the fierce glare of a summer sun now wipes a brow sprinkled over with drops of honest toil afford a rare and amusing spectacle. Now chanting his wild notes, now goading and striping the lazy bullocks plodding through the hardened mud he adds to the amusement of the sight. Rising gradually higher up the fields terminate in small hilly tracts overgrown with bushes and plants and rocky cliffs and rock-made hollows with sometimes a spring or a grove with crystal water girgling through them; and on the hill tops and along their bases are seen numerous herds of cattle grazing, some chewing the cud of sweet fancy, some eagerly crying aloud to meet their little ones lost in some dark nook or thick-set grove, while some walk on nibbling the green grass on the ground. These hills are of various dimensions verging from mere rocky elevations and rising up to the monstrous proportions. The whole land is studded over with them, but in no symmetrical order. Likewise are the various rivers and rivulets. Rivers which in the flooding season are large enough and deep enough for small vessels to plough through are seen alongside of small streamlets with reed-covered banks and the surface dotted with the leaves of the wild lotus. The weary boatman resting himself on the boatside now begins to chant his accustomed airs and eases himself from the weariness of his toil and ploughs his tiny boat through the thick-set lotus-leaves or heavy stalks of reeds growing down the margins: while the large rivers during the monsoons run roaring along fertilizing the soil through which they pass. On the surface of their waters are seen huge boats plying through the tempestuous current carrying souls frightened out of their wits and yearning to reach the further side.

The numerous clans and sub-tribes into which the Nairs, the principal inhabitants of the country, are divided furnish another striking point of resemblance between the two countries. The memory of the common descent of the clan from a common ancestress is also; kept up by the observance of death-pollution, the performance of funeral obsequies and other religious rites. The common interests of the tribe, secular or religious, are jealously guarded by the headmen who are specially convoked on great social occasions. The social delinquencies of the members of a clan or tribe are subjected to scrutiny by the clan-chieftains who arrogate to themselves all such powers. No doubt, these are all rapidly disappearing under the civilizing influences of Western refinement. Nor is the analogy between the two countries less striking with regard to the conception of devils and demons, fairies and witches, dryads and nereids. The people with the honourable exception of a few enlightened souls are firm believers in the existence of superhuman agencies in the country. The devils, as has already been explained, are midnight wanderers who seize and prey upon human beings who chance to pass through their respective jurisdictions. Hundreds of these being people of the country. Where the jurisdiction of the one ends commences that of another. Water-nymphs or nereids are located by the margins of watery grounds. The dryads are the inhabitants of trees and woods. In short the whole religion of the country is sadly corrupted by beliefs in the powers of spiritual forces.

Ireland and Irish history present similar and not less striking points of resemblance to Malabar and its history. Ireland is essentially a priest-ridden country. Its people, the great bulk of them, are immersed in the darkest depths of ignorance and superstition. With the exception of the Protestant county of Ulster, Ireland is a Roman Catholic country dominated by Roman Catholic priests who hold in their hands the keys of all social and political powers. It is said that even Parliamentary elections are surreptitiously controlled by the mystic influence which they wield over the souls of a people given over to the worst forms of superstition; and this was put forward as one of the main grounds against the late Mr. Gladstone's Home Rule

Schemes during their progress through Parliament. The superstitious Irishry are terrorized into obedience to the will of these priests, who actually stand at the gates of the unlettered and slavish electors calling down the wrath of Heaven upon those who dared to disobey their superhuman mandates. Thus even Irish Politics are under the control of these Roman Catholic priests. Such is the power which the priestly classes wield over the minds and deeds of the Irish people.

The Irish Land Question is another instance of history repeating itself in an alien clime. The land in Ireland is owned by large proprietors who tease and oppress their tenants to the uttermost. Evictions are sadly too numerous; and the lamentations of the poor Grubstreet author in the Deserted Village about a century and a quarter ago, really though not ostensibly directed against Irish landlordism, are too true even in our own day. Rack-renting has been one of the main features of the Irish Land Question. The Irish tenants have all along been a down-trodden class and the problem of the Irish land has always remained a knotty and intricate one baffling the political skill of England's greatest statesmen. All the various Land Acts passed from time to time for the amelioration of the condition of the land-holding classes in the country have proved of little or no avail; and a workable and satisfactory scheme yet remains to be devised. The Irish tenant is often fleeced to more than the annual yield of the land in the shape of rent.

Suffice it to say, that the Irish tenants are under the oppressive control of their landlords.

As an inevitable consequence of the atrocities to which the Irish landholders are subjected at the hands of the landed aristocracy we see repeated instances of plebeian uprisings in vindication of humanity and justice. The Irish are a bold and reckless class to whose unquenchable thirst of revenge are due the various outbreaks that have from time to time tarnished the pages of their national history. Precious lives have often been sacrificed at the sacred altar of social and political wrongs. People have been locked up within the prison walls for breaches of the peace; and the country has had to be constantly brought into subjection by the Coercion Acts which Parliament had to enforce against these dangerous ebullitions of fanaticism. These Coercion Acts, though aimed at in the direction of Order and Reform, have always remained, in the estimation of many a politician, a standing blot upon the fair fame and prestige of Britain's sway over Ireland. In all these various outbreaks the Land Question has figured prominently as one of the essential and predisposing causes.

In these aspects of its social life Malabar stands level with the "tortured" land of Erin. With regard to the sacerdotal supremacy detailed above it may be surmised that Malabar is equally a priest-ridden country even from its origin. The traditional history of the land is put forward justification of the plea that it belongs in exclusive monopoly to the Brahmins who form its priestly orders. They are the lords of the soil possessing large powers for oppression and domination over the labouring classes, the Nairs. All the domestic concerns of the Nairs, all their social intercourses, all their liberty of thought and action are regulated by the arbitrary will of the Brahmin priests. Not one of them, in their true religious capacity, is allowed to move his little finger except on consultation with the Brahmin priests; and disobedience to their orders is often visited with their displeasure and the resulting deprivation of their means of livelihood and banishment from society. Thus their social liberties are circumscribed and curtailed, and their sectarian privileges are narrowed and smothered by the opprobrious intervention of a priestly class who have ever remained an obstructive element in their national economy. They have been the means, and in most cases, the effective means, of thwarting and obstructing all their material, moral and social progress. Happily enough, in Malabar, owing to the direct interposition of the British Government in all its political concerns, and the absence of any appreciable francise, our political life is practically free from this vicious taint. Any large and effective representation of the people on the local Legislative Council, however much it may have been of use to us in other ways, would have been the means of producing consequences similar to those that are currently witnessed in the political history of the Emerald Isle.

Likewise as in Ireland, the land is parcelled out amongst a large landed gentry who frequently resort to the cruel practice of oppressive eviction. The rent and other dues which these proprietors called *jemmies* usually exact are mostly so exorbitant and unconscionable that the poor tenant is often unable to pay them out of the produce of the land. Failures to comply with their extortionate demands or to render willing obedience to their wishes are punished with eviction sooner or later. Various engines of oppression have been planned and adopted by them. Any birth or death in the jemmy's household or any festival or ceremony therein (and such ceremonies are numerous in Malabar) is made the occasion for an extortionate call upon the unfortunate tenant for an impossible contribution. Any social mandate oral or written issued by him or even in his name in declaration of a formal mode of action or procedure in our social sphere demands prompt and unquestioning obedience. Any costly litigation or other source of enhanced expenditure to the landlord's family is the source of a fresh drain upon the lean purse of the impoverished tenant. Any slight want of deference shown towards the person of the landlord or any member of his own household or any distant relation is the pretext for an immediate eviction of the tenant's holdings. Even disobedience to the will of the jemmy's Karistan or any member of his family is punished indirectly in like manner. This is but an inadequate account of the nature of jemmy oppression in Malabar; and none but those who have had personal experience of the same can adequately realize its full nature and extent. Corresponding to the Irish Land Acts, similar attempts have, time after time, been made in Malabar likewise, and have as often proved unavailing to produce the desired results. The Legislature has at various times endeavoured to interfere with the down-trodden condition of the Malabar tenantry by appointing commissions to draft Bills for putting an end to such evictions and legislating for the payment of reasonable compensation for unexhausted improvements. But all these have systematically proved nugatory. As in Ireland the Land Question in Malabar bristles with difficulties. And unless and until the British Legislature places an effective check upon the reckless and inhuman license of the landlord by providing for fixity of tenure, fair rent, and fair renewal fees, the condition of the masses will and must remain deplorable in the extreme.

Closely connected with this question and inevitably following from it is the question affecting the frequent fanatical outrages that do not consist with the genius of British overlordship. In this respect also the parallel with Ireland is practically complete. From A. D. 1836, *i.e.*, two years after the Coorg war, these riots have been rather too numerous and constant. In 1855 the inhuman murder of the then official head of the district was an event of stirring political importance. Closely corresponding to the Irish Coercions Acts rank our Moplah Acts which touch and concern these outbreaks. In 1859 was passed the first of such Acts, originally designed for a period of twenty years, by which it was decided to levy a fine upon all the *Amshoms* of the disturbed Taluqs through which the rioters have passed. At the end of the period it was again renewed and with the outburst of 1894 the Act was made a permanent measure and is still in force in the country. The whole country has been practically disarmed; and despite all these coercive measures these outbreaks have not been successfully stopped. One cannot resist the idea that these riots are at least partly, though not wholly, due to the oppression of the tenantry by the land-owning classes; and the possible remedies towards their eventual and permanent suppression appear to lie only in some definite scheme whereby the intellectual and moral status of the Moplah population in the backward Taluqs will be raised by means of the imparting to them of *free* and *compulsory* education, the suppression of the present defective nay dangerous system of Moplah religious instruction and the substitution in its stead of some method based upon a rational and scientific foundation, the permanent reversal of the policy of coercion and the adoption of a policy of concession, but of course within limits, in political dealings with the Moplah classes and their conciliation by other means, and last but by no means least, the final settlement of the Malabar Land Question which has all along been looming large on our legislative horizon and to which the people have been so eagerly looking forward.

CHAPTER. II

A MALABAR NAIR TARAWAD.

I do not in the present Chapter propose to deal with the origin of the Nairs of Malabar or the early history of the country about which very little is known. Nor do I propose to discuss the historical value of the many traditions current regarding these. My object is to give a brief sketch of the constitution of the Nair Tarawad as it is styled ; to describe the law of succession which prevails, the chief ceremonies performed in the Nair household, the chief national festivals celebrated ; and lastly to show how a study of the social customs of the Nairs throws light upon some of the debated questions of Comparative Jurisprudence.

The most outstanding feature in the constitution of a Malabar Nair Tarawad is that the system of kinship which obtains is one in which fathers are practically ignored and descent is reckoned through mothers. The civil law of the land takes cognisance only of relations on the female side. The constitutions of the Tarawad or family of people living together is exceedingly complex. A mother and all her children, both male and female, all her grand-children by her daughters, all her brothers and sisters and the descendants on the sister's side, in short all the woman's relatives on the female side, however distant their relationship, live together in the same block of buildings, have a common table, enjoy all her property and share it after her death in common with one another. There are, at present, instances in the country of such Tarawads with about two hundred members belonging to different branches and separated from one another by generations of descent yet all able to trace their descent from one common ancestress. When, by the constant addition of members to a Tarawad it becomes too unwieldy to be governed and managed by one man, natural forces begin to work and bring about a division of it into various distinct Tarawads which keep up the original traditions of their common descent but have no legal right to the property of one another. These partitions are often so arranged as to bring into separate Tarawads closely related members who before belonged to one branch of the original constitution and the kindred sympathies of the members are thus placed on a better and stronger basis of relationship. Over the whole of this group of members living in one Tarawad the eldest male is by legal right appointed *Karanavan* or managing head; and on his death the next senior male member, to whatever branch of the family he may belong, succeeds to that office in preference to all others. Thus the joint property of the whole Tarawad is kept under the control and management of the *Karanavan* who is legally responsible for its safe-keeping as well as for the education of its junior members and for all the necessities arising from its social status.

The Law by which succession is regulated in these Tarawads is called the Marumakkathayam law (succession by nephews.) The name Marumakkathayam is somewhat misleading since it might suggest that the family succession is restricted to nephews alone; whereas a brother or any other kinsman on the female side who happens to be the eldest male member at the time of the death of a Karanavan succeeds to the headship to the exclusion of nephews. The spirit of the law governing these Tarawads is that while the joint property belongs to the females, their natural incapacity for family government has made the eldest male member the life-trustee of the joint estate. These trustees are entitled only to maintenance out of the joint property; and must in no way alienate their trust properties without the express or tacit consent of all the members of the Tarawad; unauthorized alienation of such properties or acts of mismanagement on the part of a Karanavan being legally sufficient cause for his removal from managership and for the substitution in his stead of some one in whom the family have full confidence.

The general presumption in law is that these Karnavans have no private property of their own; anything that they might happen to possess being generally presumed to have been earned out of the incomes of the joint estates which are at the time under their management. But in case of a legal dispute if a Karanavan proves to the satisfaction of a Court-of-law that certain property is his own acquisition, such property is invariably declared his private earning. The junior members both male and female are allowed the free right of making acquisitions for themselves and these they are at absolute liberty to dispose of in any way they like, during their life time. But the private acquisitions of every member, male or female, who dies intestate lapse to the joint property and thus become the common property of the Tarawad. But of late years there has been a tendency shown by courts to declare such property to lapse to the nearest line in preference to the joint property.

The joint property thus held is impartible except with the unanimous consent of all the members, an expression of disagreement by any one single adult member, male or female, being fully sufficient for breaking off a partition arrangement. In partitions the joint property both moveable and immoveable is divided in equal shares; but the Karanavan for the time being has a conventional right to a double share. Should a Karanavan by reason of his distant relationship to some particular branch of the family or through preference for his own immediate branch deprive the former of the benefits that are derivable from their legal claim to the joint property such a branch has the privilege of suing him for maintenance and getting a decree for the same against him.

With regard to the question of succession another thing to be noticed is that in the absence of any male member to succeed to the office of Karanavan the eldest female takes precedence of all others; and when a Tarawad becomes extinct on the death of the last surviving member, the property is claimed by the reversioners of the Tarawad or in the absence of even such heirs escheated to Government.

I now come to speak of Nair Marriage customs. Marriage ties are somewhat loose amongst the Nairs. There are, in the first place, a great variety of social considerations to be satisfied before a marriage can be effected The people, though consisting of one dominant class which goes under the wide denomination of Nairs, are yet split up into close on a hundred castes with very minute social distinctions separating them. Each of these separate castes generally consists of a number of families which may be collectively styled a *clan*. These families constituting the clan are all related to one another by community of pollution and as such are considered quasi-relationships to one another. Hence intermarriages between the members of the same clan are socially prohibited. Among the various clans some are socially superior or inferior to others; and some there are which maintain equality of social standing with one another. Now the only socially valid marriages are those in which the parties belong to the last mentioned class or those in which the bridegroom belongs to a clan superior to that to which the bride belongs. Those clans which are on the same social level may be together named a *tribe*. In all other cases the union entails social stigma upon the fame and dignity of the bride's family; and it not unfrequently happens that the family is socially ostracised. There are still nicer social distinctions which in certain cases are made to operate as obstructions in the way of marriages even when the parties happen to belong to the same class. But with the spread of western notions and modes of thought scruples about these minor caste differences are fast disappearing. But all the same one peculiarity remains to be noticed. In the extreme South of British Malabar, there are instances of marriages contracted between a high-caste bride and a low-caste bridegroom. In such cases the husband does not touch the wife when she is engaged in taking her meals.

There is, in fact, no fixed rule or custom as to marriages in Malabar. They are terminable at the will of either party and the law takes no notice of them. No religious element enters into the performance of a marriage and there does not exist one generally adopted etiquette in the matter. The ceremonies if they may be so-called vary in the different parts of the country; and a union though effected and socially recognized in the most public manner possible does not in any way possess legal force or validity. There is no law of divorce or maintenance governing the married couples. Wife and children do not possess the legal privilege of claiming maintenance from the father who is invariably looked upon as a useless legal factor in Nair society. It is also curious to observe that a wife ceases to have any connexion with her husband's *Tarawad* after his death. Long established custom requires that she must quit her husband's house for her own as soon as he has drawn his last breath; and that she must never after come back to it even in cases of the direst necessity. But provided she happens to be the daughter of some deceased *Karanavan* of her husband, this difficulty can, on that plea, be got over; and she may come to the husband's house without prejudice to her social position in her capacity of a daughter of a former member of the family.

It is customary in Malabar for a wife to avoid mentioning the name of her husband. In cases of necessity he is usually called 'the father' of some one of her children or by some such euphemistic term. It is looked upon as a breach of female decorum to indulge in such prohibited forms of address.

With regard to the naming of children the one interesting point to be observed is that they are usually, with but few exceptions, named after their parents or some deceased ancestor of the *Tarawad*, male or female, as the case may be. Thus the Nair names met within the country at the present day have most of them come down from the earliest times. But when once a child is thus named the members of the *Tarawad* have an instinctive reluctance to use the name for the child, for it would call up the dear memories and associations of that ancestor after whom the child has been named. It is then called in many cases by some pet name.

The naming ceremony takes place on the twenty-eighth day after birth or in certain other places, at some auspicious moment and on some auspicious day in the sixth month.

An advanced section of the community had of late years been pressing for legislative interference in Nair marriages; and Mr. C. Sankara Nair, a prominent and worthy member of the community, some years ago, introduced into the local Legislative Council a measure for legalizing such marriages. It was intended in effect to strike at the root of some at least of those traditions and usages, which, however much they commend themselves to the orthodox, are ill-adapted to the conditions of the present day. Naturally it evoked much opposition, though curiously enough the opposition came from educated men. It is impossible to account for this except on the ground of unwillingness on the part of these men to make public the inner aspects of their social life. Malabar society is still a mystery to the civilized world. No accurate and systematic elucidation of its nature and working is extant. However, a fair majority strongly espoused the main principles of the Bill. A commission was appointed by Government to investigate the matter; and it sat in almost all the principal centres of the district collecting evidence from all available sources. The final expression of opinion by the members was, in spirit, favourable to the reformers. It was reported by the commission that the existing systems had no religious sanction or authority to back them up; in which case there could be no objections of a religious nature in the way of legislation; and that legislation was, under the circumstances, a necessity. They thought, however, that the country was not yet ripe for such sweeping and revolutionary measures as those advocated by the reform party, and indicated certain fresh lines of action upon which they recommended legislation. On the ground of its ultra-radical nature the original Bill was thrown out; but subsequently another Bill on the lines recommended by the commission was framed by Mr. Sankara Nair and was sometime ago passed into law by the Madras Legislature.

It seemed strange that the Bill should have been opposed by educated men. It is high time that some efforts were made to place the Nairs on a basis of equality with the enlightened nations of the world. The effects of western education have already begun to manifest themselves in the land. The manifold superstitions that block the path of national progress are rapidly vanishing off the face of the country. Time is on the side of the reformers. It is impossible to resist the progressive movement. It may be perfectly true that under the customs and usages that now obtain amongst us our ancestors fared well. But the customs and usages that suited the people of a by-gone age can scarcely suit us who live amid very different surroundings. Our progress as a nation must become an impossibility if we are compelled to regulate our social life by customs that are antiquated. It should be the central aspiration in the life of every nation to raise itself in all possible ways and not rest satisfied with the national immobility of a China

> "For unless above himself he can
> Erect himself, how poor a thing is man."

However legislative remedies are being adopted towards the social elevation of the people. The most fundamental error into which the opponents of the Bill floundered consisted in their mixing up what is usually known as Kettu Kallianam with the kind of marriage which the reformers sought to legalize.

(For a description of Kettu Kallianam, *Vide* Chapter on the same.)

The union of man and woman goes by variety of designations in the different parts of Malabar. Such are Sambandham, Kidakkura Kallianam, Pudamuri, Uzhamporukkal and others. But in not one of these is there the faintest shadow of a religious element. The ways in which unions are effected and the formalities observed also differ in different places. In some parts of the country, when all the necessary social conditions are satisfied the marriage is talked of and arranged by, the *Tarawad* people of both parties usually the Karanavans; and an auspicious day is fixed for the consummation. On the evening of the appointed day, a near relation of the bridegroom, along with a few others repairs to the bride's house taking with him a supply of cloths of divers sorts and materials for chewing, such as betel-leaves, tobacco, and areca nuts; and also a certain sum of money for meeting incidental expenses. Shortly after they reach the house, the bridegroom starts thither with a select few of his friends. A good supper is provided at the bride's house at the cost of the bride's people. In some parts the supper is preceded by the serving of a course of of eatables. But in other parts this is not done. At supper all are seated on mats together. Presents of cloths are given by the bride's people to the servants and attendants of the bridegroom (men of high position who may happen to be with him, being of course omitted for personal reasons) and *vice versa.* Then in the presence of the assembled guests the cloths are taken by the bridegroom and given to the bride who accepts them with alacrity. Money-offerings are also made to Brahmins who may be present on the occasion. Thus the marriage ceremony is consummated. There are, as I have stated before, local differences in the various details that complete the ceremony; for example, in some places the giving of the cloths to the bride by the bridegroom is postponed till after the expiry of six months from that time; in others the ceremony is conducted on a very grand scale. But none of these possess any solemn or binding character. The description given has special reference to the southern parts of the district. In the eastern parts the celebration is on a very grand scale,—and even dowries are given by the bride's people. In North Malabar the sacredness of marital ties is rigidly observed; and it may be said that fathers amongst the Northerners keep and maintain the children and their mother out of the former's family all through their lives. With the widening of men's thoughts the details of the ceremony are undergoing desirable modifications.

The members of a clan which keeps up the memory of their once common descent are all bound together by community of pollution. If a member of any one family of a clan dies, his death brings pollution upon all the members of all the families composing that clan. It lasts for fifteen days and it shuts out all the members of the clan from all social intercourse and dealings with members of stranger clans. On the morning of the fifteenth day the members of the clan have to be purified from pollution by a mixture of oil, water and cowdung thrown three times on their backs by a class of people who go by different denominations in different parts of the country. In the case of the death of a child below the age of puberty the pollution rules are not very stringently enforced. In this case social intercourse with stranger clans is freely allowed. The purification on the fifteenth day requires only a bath in a tank. As in the case of death-pollution the birth of a child in any case likewise brings pollution on the rest of a clan for a period of fifteen days; in this case, however, the rules are not even so rigorous as in the case of the death of a child below the age of puberty. The only restriction is that the members of the clan are not allowed to worship inside sacred temples during the fifteen days; and there is no purification rite strictly so-called. But the child's mother has to observe the pollution to much the same extent as she would have to do in the case of a regular death pollution.

The chief household ceremonies enjoined on the Nair families are many in number. Some of them are historically important in that they point to the prevalence even in our own day of ancestor-worship in the country.

(For a description of 'Ancestor-worship' *Vide* Chapter on "Some Phases of Religious Life.")

The attainment of puberty by a girl is publicly announced by the celebration of a ceremony called Thirandu Kallianam, which is also accompanied with a feasting of guests. The girl has to bathe on the fourth day with the help of the *Enangar* females; and after that what is called a *Pattu* has to be celebrated. Of course, feasting is an inevitable accompaniment of this. This *Pattu* consists in certain ballads sung by the *Mannans*, a peculiar class privileged for the same. He is rewarded by the *Enangars* and the relations of the girl. This *Pattu* may be celebrated on any night from the fifth day onwards, and within the month or some time after that. The details differ in the various parts of the country.

Another ceremony enjoined by the custom of the country is called *Pulikudi*. This is generally performed about the delivery period (usually the ninth month) of the first pregnancy of a woman. Like every other household ceremony this is also accompanied with a costly feast. The principal feature about this is, that at an auspicious moment on some auspicious day, the girl is made to drink, after some ceremonials, a peculiar kind of mixture made of tamarind juice and other flavor-giving substances in the presence of guests. The mixture is usually poured into her mouth by one or more of her relatives. The exact motive or utility of this is yet unknown.

The three great national festivals are *Onam*, *Vishu*, and *Thiruvathira*. (For their description *Vide* Chapters on these.)

Relics of polygamy are still preserved amongst the Nairs; and polyandry may be said to be in practice in a modified form and in exceptional instances. In tracing the various stages of marriage McLennan makes mention of two forms of polyandry, *viz.*, that which obtains amongst the Nairs where the husbands are strangers to each other and that in which the husbands are brothers. This statement requires to be corrected and modified. Though in ancient times polyandry must have been prevalent amongst the Nairs, it has for a long time ceased to be a recognized feature of Nair life. The forms of polyandry now obtaining are 'exceptional and sporadic'. Forms of the first kind of polyandry *viz.*, that in which the husbands are strangers are found in some places not yet brought under the influences of civilization; and those of the second in which the husbands are brothers obtain amongst the barber classes, who are themselves Nairs but who have fallen from their social estate by the degrading nature of their profession *viz.*, shaving. Such instances are common enough. But polyandry obtains amongst the Nairs proper only in very rare cases and in particular localities. Such forms also obtain amongst the Tiyya classes and there is no social stain attached to this custom amongst either these *barbers* or Tiyyas. With regard to polygamy it has been noticed that it still prevails amongst the Nairs; and the want of legislative restrictions among them lends decided support to its continuance. Exogamy is rigidly enforced. As I have already pointed out, no man is allowed to marry a girl from among the members of his own *clan* for fear of social excommunication. But this strictness in the matter of Exogamy, seems to be due, not as McLennan thinks, to the scarcity of women, nor to female infanticide but, as Tylor conjectures, to an innate sense of the physiological evils of in-breeding.

In speaking of household ceremonies I have dwelt at some length upon what may reasonably be styled ancestor-worship. Dead ancestors are deified and offerings are in some families made to their spirits; and sometimes even idols are set up for them to be worshipped as the abode of the deities. I am not however prepared to maintain that this is a universal practice amongst the Nairs. But in certain *Tarwads* it undoubtedly prevails. Besides ancestor-worship, animal-worship, tree-worship, devil-worship and serpent-worship are not uncommon.

(*Vide* Chapter, on "Religious Life," for these kinds of worship; and Chapter on serpent-worship for the same.)

(For the religious institutions such as the *Pana* and *Para* and *Desapattu, Vide* Chapter on "Religious Life.")

Certain aspects of our social life are of importance from a juristic point of view. They throw light upon a question of Comparative Jurisprudence about which the great jurist Sir H. Maine allowed himself to be drawn away into an apparent blunder. He maintained that the Patriarchal System was the primitive and earliest stage in the development of the family and that all others obtaining at the present day are but developments from this system. This theory found universal acceptance with jurists until the publication of McLennan's '*Primitive Marriage*' and Prof. Bachoofen's *Mutterrecht* effectually showed it to be wrong. In the former work it was evidence chiefly collected from Australia and aboriginal America, proving the existence there of organizations in which succession is regulated through the female side and fathers are looked upon as insignificant elements in the progress of society which helped to dissipate the error. Now it has been shown that the system of kinship which obtains in the Nair families (the same is the case with the families of some other castes) is also one in which the fathers are practically ignored and descent is reckoned through mothers. And further there has been no period in the history of Malabar when a system of kinship obtained amongst the Nairs which makes the smallest approach to Maine's Patriarchal System. Hence the study of

Nair society helps to disprove Maine's theory quite as much as the evidence that was obtained, after years of laborious research, from pre-Columbian America.

CHAPTER III.

MARUMAKKATHAYAM.

In the preceding chapter I gave a brief account of a Malabar Nair Tarawad. I there pointed out that the law by which succession is regulated in these Tarawads is called the Marumakkathayam law, Marumakkathayam being a term applied to that system of kinship which regulates succession through the maternal line. It is a system which obtains in all parts of the world which have not yet emerged from primitive social obscurity, and is not peculiar to Malabar alone. It marks a stage through which all races, however high up in the scale of progress now, must, in the infancy of their social existence, have passed. Our own times present instances of its wide prevalence. Most Australian tribes of the present day preserve it in its pure form. America, by furnishing McLennan and others with examples of societies based upon systems similar to the Marumakkathayam has rendered material assistance in the refutation of the Patriarchal Theory set up by Sir H. Maine. Across the Himalayan border Tibet is said to maintain a system which is only one stage in advance of it. The Lycians mentioned by Herodotus followed practically the same system. This widespread law of female descent lies rather deep in the history of society; and though the nations of Europe and most of the nations of Asia have long given it up for better and more refined systems very many societies at the present day preserve a maternal system of descent.

An important question for consideration and one which has not been satisfactorily solved by any one, concerns the origin of this system in Malabar. Various theories have been advanced in regard to this. But there are two which stand out from the rest by reason of their being in a manner free from objection. The first of these may be called the "Brahminic Theory." According to this theory, the origin of Marumakkathayam is ascribed to the Numbudri Brahmins of Malabar. These people, the date of whose arrival in Malabar has not yet been settled, brought with them their own civilization and social laws. When they colonized the country, Malabar is said to have been a jungly tract, for the most part unfit for habitation. There are some, however, who hold the view that Malabar in remote antiquity was submerged deep under water, and that it must have been saved from the Arabian Sea by eruption of some hidden volcanic peak. But whatever the historical value of these conjectures may be, it is now conceded by all antiquarians that in the course of its history Malabar has received two distinct bands of immigrants, differing widely in their customs and manners, language and social organisation. The question as to which of these came first is quite foreign to the purpose of this treatise. One set of these colonists is identified with the Brahmins of Malabar, usually called Numbudries. They are known to belong to the Aryan race of mankind; and they preserve to this day racial and national peculiarities which testify to an Aryan origin. The other band of immigrants is generally believed to be of the Dravidian family, and forms the recognized stem of the Nair Branch of the Malayalies. The Aryan Brahmins when they came into the country had the same social organization as exists among their successors of to-day. Their laws strictly ordain that only the eldest member of a household shall be left free to enter lawful wedlock with a woman of their own caste, the younger members being left to shift for themselves in this matter. In ancient times the only asylum which these latter could find in the existing state of their social circumstances was in the Nair families which settled round about them. It should, in this connexion, be remembered that the Brahmins formed an aristocratic order; and as such they were the exclusive custodians and expositors of the law. Naturally enough, too, large numbers of Brahmin younger sons, who were looking about for wives, turned to the Nair families, and began to enter into illegitimate unions of the nature of concubinage. Now the sanctity of formal and religious marriages was incompatible with the looseness and degradation involved in these illegitimate unions; and Brahmin ingenuity discovered a ready means of getting over the difficulty by a social prohibition of all valid marriages among the Nairs, which would otherwise have prejudicially interfered with their conjugal destinies. Moreover, the permission of valid marriages among the Nairs would have necessitated on their part a legitimate acknowledgment of sonship and parentage, which had they sanctioned it, would have injured their own interests in regard to the inheritance of property. They would in that case have had to alter the nature of their family succession. Such property considerations were mainly at the basis of this social enactment on the part of the Brahmins. Their object would have been defeated if the junior members of their families had been allowed to contract lawful marriages, whether with their own kinsfolk or with the Nair women. This would have involved a superfluous and unwieldy addition to their families. The maintenance and support of these numerous progeny would have resulted in the dissipation of their property. Reasons such as these led to the restriction of their own lawful marriages. To enforce this social edict upon the Nairs the Brahmins made use of the powerful weapon of their aristocratic ascendancy in the country; and the Nairs readily submitted to the Brahmin supremacy. Thus it came about that the custom of concubinage so freely indulged in by the Brahmins with Nair women obtained such firm hold upon the country that it has only been strengthened by the lapse of time. At the present day there are families, especially in the interior of the district, who look upon it as an honor to be thus united with Brahmins. But a reaction has begun to take place against this feeling; and Brahmin alliances are invariably looked down upon in respectable Nair Tarawads. This reactionary feeling took shape in the Malabar Marriage Act.

A second and less commonly accepted theory in regard to the origin of Marumakkathayam is what may be called the 'Property Theory.' According to this theory the system was instituted in order to secure the property of the Nair families *in tact.* A system of valid marriages and male kinship would have meant partition and consequent dissipation of property in these families; and having this in view, the founders of the system declared property impartible which would have been impossible had the system of kinship been reckoned exclusively in the male line.

A new and more plausible theory, and one which has amply been corroborated by the history of nations, is to be found in the practice of polyandry which obtains among many nations even in our own day. In the primitive stages of society, the indiscriminate union of the sexes forms the sole feature of married life. As societies, progress, men's views on marriage broaden, and polyandry comes to prevail. This gives place to polygamy and finally monogamy is adopted. This is the way in which McLennan traces the successive stages of marriage. Now in the first two stages *viz.*, promiscuity and polyandry, paternity is practically indeterminate; for in the first the offspring of women belong by common right to a number of men who form the husband class; and in polyandry likewise a woman's children belong on the father's side to a number of men together, though on the mother's side they belong to one and the same individual. Owing to the absence of any marks of distinction it is impossible to determine paternity and so the devolution of property cannot be prescribed to the sons and in the male line but must be prescribed in some line and to some persons that are clearly distinguishable. Such persons are best found in the sons of sisters who, as *nephews*, are determinate identities even though on account of the uncertainty of their parentage they are not so determinate as *sons*. Thus the ready and unobjectionable expedient was hit upon by which nephews, and by necessary consequence sisters, were created the rightful heirs to a man's property instead of his wife and children. Hence arose the custom of female descent of property.

I pointed out in the previous chapter that polyandry in its simplest and essential form *viz.*, that of one woman having more than one husband at a time is still prevalent in parts of Malabar, and that no social stigma attaches to it. The following is what the Malabar Marriage Bill Commission has to say on the subject of polyandry in Malabar:—" If by polyandry we simply mean a usage which permits a female to cohabit with a plurality of lovers without loss of caste, social degradation, or disgrace, then we apprehend that this usage is distinctly sanctioned by Marumakkathyam; and that there are localities where, and classes amongst whom, this license is still availed of." The late Sir. T. Muthusami Iyer says on this self-same subject:—"Apart from negative and symbolic evidence there is positive evidence to show that polyandry still lingers in the Ponnany and Walluvanad Taluques, especially on the Cochin frontier of the former Taluque." It is a fair inference from this that polyandry was once universal in Malabar, and that out of it sprang the great institution of Marumakkathayam.

And this inference is borne out by Mr. Grose who, in his "Travels to the East Indies," an old book published before 1762 A. D., says as follows:—

"It is among them (the Nairs) that principally prevails the strange custom of one wife being common to a number: in which point the great power of custom is seen from its rarely or never producing any jealousies or quarrels among the co-tenants of the same woman. Their number is not so much limited by any specific law, as by a kind of tacit convention, it scarce ever happening that it exceeds six or seven. The woman however is under no obligation to admit above a single attachment though not less respected for using her privilege to its utmost extent. If one of the husbands happens to come to the house when she is employed with another he knows that circumstance by certain signals left at the door that his turn is not come and departs very resignedly."

In this connexion it is worth while observing that the prevalence of polyandry may in its turn justify the conclusion that there was in our country a period when promiscuous intercourse prevailed. Thus it is quite possible that Marumakkathayam may have arisen out of the earliest form of marriage *viz.*, promiscuity, though there is no direct evidence of this promiscuity except in its probable descendant, polyandry, which has lasted down to our own times.

Sir John Lubbock says that the natural progress of ideas among mankind is that in the primitive period, when men lived in hordes, the child naturally belonged to the *clan*. This stage is in practice identical with the stage of promiscuity or of polyandry, in which a number of fathers collectively own the offspring of a woman. The process of time and the change of circumstances tend to vest the ownership of children not in the *clan* but in the *mother*. This is also parallel with the former stage; but with this difference, that in this stage the superiority of the woman's right to the child's person over that of the *clan* is gradually becoming recognized. The stage of polyandry, no doubt, is an advance on that of promiscuity. In the latter there is no distinction of wives whatever. But in the former the wives begin to be isolated. The effect of both upon the establishment of parentage is practically the same. In polygamy both paternity and maternity are ascertained; but it is nevertheless regarded as an unsatisfactory state of social life, though it is a far more advanced state than polyandry. Now from ownership by the mother the children pass on to ownership by the father, which is manifestly a more refined system. Then in course of time the child becomes the common property of the father and the mother,—the principle that prevails to-day in civilized life and is co-existent with monogamy and settled marriage.

Thus it has been shown that the real origin of our Marumakkathayam is to be sought in the system of polyandry or if we go a step further back, in promiscuity, which marks the dawn of married life. I know that there are many who would object to this theory and would assign as the origin of this system the racial pride and necessity of the Brahmin aristocracy. For my own part I am inclined to think—and there are others who would think with me,—that polyandry or promiscuity must have been its real origin. Of course there is no denying the fact that in a comparatively later stage, our social life after it had come under Brahminic influence was greatly affected by its perverse tendencies. McLennan, Lubbock and Mayor and other European writers agree that Marumakkathayam could only have originated from a type of polyandry resembling free love. Mr. Wigram, a Judge of considerable Malabar experience says:—"I am quite ready to admit that but for the Brahmins, all traces of polyandry would long since have disappeared and that the Brahmins encouraged concubinage between the younger members of their family and the

Nair women for the purpose of maintaining the impartibility of their estates." With this, however, I am not here immediately concerned. But for my faith in this theory I would not have ventured to put forward our Marumakkathayam as being sufficient evidence in refutation of the Patriarchal theory maintained by Sir Henry Maine. If it had been the result of an arbitrary caprice on the part of the Numbudri Brahmins it could not have possibly supported my position in regard to the "earliest and universal" nature of that theory.

The theory, that polyandry is the origin of Marumakkathayam has been combated on a ground which will not bear scrutiny. If, it is said, the system of female kinship were the gradual outgrowth from a primitive and widely prevalent custom such as polyandry, then it would be more rational to suppose that the system would have been preserved amongst the Parayas, Pulayas, Naidis and other depressed races of Malabar who are generally accepted as its unquestioned aborigines. But as a matter of fact these people follow Makkathayam and hence, the improbability of the theory is rendered all the greater. The critics, however, seem to forget one important point in our national history. It has been universally admitted that the Nairs are Dravidian immigrants and that they brought with them their own civilization. Looking at the matter in this light there seems to be no great necessity for the supposition that their customs were identical with those of the people of the country into which they immigrated. The

Nairs developed the system of female descent in their original northern abodes, and when they immigrated south they carried the system to Malabar. The aboriginal inhabitants had also developed this system, but owing to the absence in their case of extraneous influence, such as that of the Numbudris in our case, they had outlived it. In the case of the Nairs there can be no doubt that the Numbudri domination in the country has helped very much to maintain the custom in tact for such a long period of time without alteration. They had such power in the land —and they still have—as to enable them to prolong at their will even more important and far-reaching institutions than these. Moreover, it seems reasonable to suppose that polyandry, from which the system of female kinship has sprung in other parts of the world such as Australia, and America should have been the origin of a similar custom in Malabar.

As the habits of the individual change with its growth so do the institutions of nations vary with their development. A nation in its infancy, adopts systems which suit its life as it exists then. We see around us that the importance of maternity over paternity is maintained only by those races of mankind still struggling in the infancy of social life. Marumakkathayam is a primitive institution instinctively adopted by nations in early times.

On this score it may be and has been argued that every innovation upon it would only result in national discomfort and dissatisfaction, as when the old furniture of a house is replaced by new. I should readily subscribe to this argument were it not for my belief in the Universal law which guides all nations and prepares them for the struggles of this life—I mean the law of progress. Nations have always changed their ideas and institution, through imperceptible gradations, according to their views of general expediency and progress. They have thrown away primitive traditions and customs to adapt themselves to modified environments. In the race of mankind, the law of progress and of change even in customs, however good and wholesome, must be given precedence over all other laws. We cannot check it by arbitrary restraints. We should never lose sight of the eternal truth that

> "The old order changeth, yielding place to new,
> And God fulfils himself in many ways
> Lest one good custom should corrupt the world.

This is an age of progress, an age of revolution, in which one form of society is rapidly passing away, and its place being filled up by better forms fashioned after western models. Usages regarded as wholesome and sacred a few years ago are now practically defunct and obsolete. Fashions of dress and manners and modes of living and thought are likewise passing through the crucible of Western civilization. Reason is beginning to be the guide instead of blind adherance to customs. Changes in society will come about whether purposely introduced or not. Men's minds are becoming imbued with refined conceptions of life.

Thus it seems hardly inconsistent with prudence and policy to introduce changes, not of course radical in nature but slow and in the long run, desirable. In the existing state of our society it is not possible to introduce sweeping changes by legislative measures; for no such sudden reformation is possible in our world where nature works slowly and one cannot see the growth of a flower. Changes must be slow and must proceed from within, as was the case with English Constitution. Thus it was that the growth of popular sentiment found practical expression in the Malabar Marriage Act. It was a measure that came forth from within and not imposed from without; and so it richly deserves to be treated with all respect and consideration.

Another part of the subject is concerned with *marriages.* On this as well as on the subject of property observations have already been made in foregoing chapter. Many educated Malayalees, who ought to know better, seem to labour under the mistaken impression that Malabar Marumakathayam marriages are quite as formal and religious as marriages in any other part of the world. On the subject of marriage in general Sir Fitz-James Stephen says:—" Most people regard marriage as a contract and something more; But I never heard of any one who denied that it is at all events a contract and by far the most important of all contracts. It is certainly not regarded in this country in all cases as a contract between the persons married as it is in Europe, but it certainly is regarded as a contract between some persons—the parents of the parties or the parents of the girl and the husband. Whatever words we choose to employ, it is clear that all the elements of a contract must from the very nature of the case be found wherever a marriage occurs. There must be an agreement; there must be a consideration for that agreement; and there must be as a consequence a set of correlative rights and duties." Thus it will be seen that a marriage is in the main a contract though not always unaccompanied by some other element. In the highest acceptation of the term it is a contract solemnized by a religious sanction. Thus there are two sides to a marriage a *legal* and a *religious*. Now in the case of our marriages both these elements are wanting. They are not *legal* because they do not create any correlative rights and duties, and because in the majority of cases there is no agreement between the contracting parties; in which connection it should be observed that adultery is no offence amongst us, though even amongst the Hottentots and Australians it is judged worthy of being visited with the extreme penalty of the law. So also we have no law of divorce or maintenance. Bigamy and kindred offences are not recognized as crimes under the Indian Penal Code. Thus the *legal* side is absolutely wanting. So also the *religious* side. The late Sir T. Muthusami Iyer, again, says in regard to the religious nature of our marriages:—" They are not regarded as constituting a religious ceremony or Samskaram or Sacrament in the Hindu or European sense of the term. There is no officiating priest in attendance: there is no formula to be repeated; there is no Vedic, Puranic, or religious chant or exhortation and there is no formal benediction." These weighty remarks show to a certainty that our marriages are in no way religious.

The joint family system so peculiar to Malabar is a much cherished element in the institution of Marumakkathayam. It is no doubt a time-honored system which the majority of a people yet clinging to the old old order of things would be entirely averse to modifying, much less abandoning. Nevertheless time requires its modification though not its absolute surrender. It has been in the past few years working much mischief owing to the incongruity existing between its principles and the altered ideas of the people.

Under the Marumakkathayam system property cannot be divided unless all the members of a Tarawad, come to a unanimous agreement. Under the system as it is administered at present, the Karanavan or manager obtains practically all power in the Tarawad. I am not advocating a total abolition of the system at present. I freely concede that it has its use in the way of preserving the stability of the family property, and that its wholesale effacement might result for the time in hardships to the people. But its tremendous disadvantages greatly outweigh its small advantages.

The system as it now exists, carries with it many drawbacks and evils. It requires to be altered so as to suit the existing conditions of our life. The main objections that can be taken to it are of supreme importance in our national economy. We have already seen that its existence was due to causes which are fast disappearing from the country. Polygamy and polyandry are being rapidly abandoned. Female descent of property, being due to the indeterminate nature of paternity, must yield place to descent in the male line when the causes for the former are disappearing by the establishment of settled marriages. The tendency is daily increasing with us to look to the interests of wife and children and place them on a level of affection which has had no parallel in our social history before. Thus, though a thorough change might, in the existing state of our society, only paralyse its energies some change would be justified by the exigencies of the times. I do not believe that there are many leaders in the country capable of independent and sound judgment who would advocate the retention of an outworn and impracticable institution such as the Tarawad system is. It may be that many of these may be satisfied with its modification on lines warranted by our present circumstances. But, sooner or later a time will come when every phase of our life and society will have so completely changed as to demand another system based on healthier and sounder principles.

The system as it is administered to-day fosters a dangerous spirit of idleness amongst the members of the joint family. They are perfectly certain that their vested rights in the joint property will supply them with all the necessaries of life whether they apply their own labour and capital in the management and upkeep of it or not. The law is ready to help them in case of their being refused maintenance by an arbitrary Karanavan.

There is also the obvious fact that the probable discontent of the junior members regarding the Karanavan's management may lead to constant quarrels in the family. It is not too much to say that such family dissensions are likely to give rise to numberless litigations. Of late years the number of litigations consequent on the careless actions of Karanavans has been increasing by leaps and bounds; and many a wealthy Tarawad has been practically ruined. How can we expect any harmony of life or any unity of purpose to prevail amongst members who belong to diverse and distant branches, with little or nothing to keep them in sympathy with each other especially in these days when the interests of one's sisters and one's wife are diametrically opposed in every way? While the former are engaged in looking after the interests of their own children who are to inherit their brother's earnings, the latter will be doing everything in her power to promote those of her own children who as children of her husband are left outside the pale of their father's protection after his decease. Thus the current of domestic life is never allowed to run smooth.

It is also a fact worthy of notice that a family disturbed by dissensions due chiefly to the lax operations of the joint property system loses its prestige in the eyes of neighbouring families. In addition to civil actions criminal proceedings are very often the outcome of such quarrels. The members of such a disturbed family cannot have any peace of mind, being worried incessantly by the thought of litigation and anxiety as to how they may obtain the support of adherents from other branches of the family. Such are some of the evils that arise when a Karanavan violates the trust reposed in him as the unquestioned trustee of the joint estate. This evil is all the more patent when the Karanavan happens to have no line of members standing in an intimate relation to him.

Moreover, the system often leads to injustice being done by the Karanavan to the other members of the family who are equally with himself entitled to all the benefits accruing from the joint property. The eldest member by virtue of his birth-right retains the power of management; and if he proves troublesome or offensive, as very often he does, the difficulty of checking his malpractices renders the position of the other members all the worse. The conduct of such a Karanavan thus deprives the other claimants of the family of their legitimate right.

Again, the hostile attitude of the junior members that I have adverted to towards a Karanavan and his colleagues in his unrighteous proceedings, naturally makes him less interested in the welfare of the Tarawad estates; and tends to careless cultivation and the resulting impoverishment of the landed estates. It naturally inclines the balance of his affection in favour of his wife and children, to whose cause he becomes all the more jealously attached. Thus the joint family system is working its way towards the practical substitution of a paternal instead of a maternal line of descent. This is nearly the stage in which we are now situated. This practical substitution requires some sanction in the popular estimation. This sanction cannot, in our case, be *religious*; for the religious doctrines enjoined by Sankara Acharyar our great lawgiver, strictly uphold the existing system. Besides, those doctrines, claiming as they do, a divine origin are unalterable. Such a sanction must proceed from a determinate source whose mandates the people will have to obey despite their religious idiosyncrasies. The time of sacerdotal dictation is long past. Political power has taken the place of the old religious authority. Hence the command of a political superior alone will be adequately obeyed and acted up to by the people. Hence the necessity for an Act to sanction the adoption of a custom which has already begun to be favored.

The system as it stands at present, by not giving the members separately free and ample scope to contend against the growing keenness of competition, obstructs the progress of industries. Stimulation of industries is obviously impossible under a system in which the members have no individual interests save those created by force of circumstances, and in which they cannot claim their separate shares of their property, which they might safely invest and utilize in such industries. This system, besides, is wholly unsuited to the present age, which is an age of individual ownership of property. Tribal and family ownership have all been given up by all surrounding nations; the retention of this system would be tantamount to the deliberate arrest of our national development.

I cannot better close this chapter than by quoting here the eloquent words in which the Malabar Marriage Bill Commissioners who are the latest authorities on the existing usages and customs of the country have expressed their opinion of this obnoxious system :—"With the advance of education Marumakkathayam is becoming hopelessly unworkable. It offends against every principle of political economy and of healthy family life. It is based upon the doctrine that there is no merit in female virtue and no sin in unchastity; and of this doctrine the very founders of this system are heartily ashamed. By freeing a man from the obligation of maintaining his wife and offspring it sanctions the reckless propagation of the species, destroying all motives of prudence and forethought, and forces up the population to the point whence it must be put down by the actual want of the means of subsistence."

CHAPTER IV.

LOCAL TRADITIONS AND SUPERSTITIONS.

The history of the world shows that the earliest stages of society are characterized by blind faith in the supernatural and the fabulous. Our society has not yet reached a very advanced stage of development and it is therefore no matter for surprise that superstitions and traditions of a mythical nature exert a powerful influence upon the lives of the people of Malabar. It is the purpose of this chapter to give an account of some of these traditions and superstitions.

I begin with the tradition concerning the origin of Malabar itself which centres round the person of Parasu Rama. But it has already been described in the beginning of the chapter on "Thoughts on Malabar." Hence I do not propose to deal with it here a second time.

Mythical accounts of demons and monsters are very common in Malabar. There are in parts of the country old dilapidated buildings, wells, and tanks of which no one knows the makers or builders. They are ascribed by the common people to laborers of the demon class who existed in the country in very early times, and who went by the name of *Bhuthathanmar*. The accounts given of these beings are very curious. Herculean labors are attributed to them.

They are believed to be a kind of 'midnight wanderers' under a demon-chief who regulates and directs their night-work. They must not go out in the day time; but must shut themselves up from human gaze. Any work entrusted to them has to be completed before the break of day; and should any piece of work be only half-finished in the morning it is religiously left in its unfinished condition. Also if, in the course of their work, these demons are seen by any human being they have to leave off at once in whatever stage of progress the work may happen to be at the time. They are also said to have undertaken many pieces of work in one and the same night; and sometimes in these cases also their work, especially the last item to which they have put their hands has had to remain unfinished owing to the approach of day. Such is the popular explanation of the many uncompleted pieces of architecture that are still to be seen in parts of the country. The demons are supposed to work from a natural and irresistible impulse; and they give their services gratis at the bidding of their chief. They all mess together at the chief's residence, and are in no wise troublesome elements in the population of the country. Of their origin next to nothing is known; but they are believed to have come into the world as full grown demons. Even now they are not an extinct race; but the conditions of their existence are pitiable indeed. On one occasion after completing the construction of a building they went to their chief, as was their wont, to ask for fresh work. Having completed the task assigned to them they again went to their chief and asked for more work. They did this time after time, and annoyed their chief, who was engaged in a game of chess. In order to get rid of them, the chief directed them to go and count the number of waves in the ocean. On this mission they immediately proceeded not knowing that they could never accomplish their task. Thus the chief was enabled to apply himself to the game without interruption. But the demons to their utter bewilderment soon found out that their new work was never ending. Obedient, however, to the mandate of their leader they would not relinquish the work. They went on counting and are to this day believed to be engaged in the hopeless task of counting the ocean waves.

In some parts of the country there are huge upright blocks of granite around which have clustered certain pathetic traditions. These are especially met with in hilly parts abounding in rocks. Such tracts of country are generally believed to be the abode of evil spirits; and the upright blocks of stone are supposed to be the bodies of evil spirits, which became petrified because the spirits slighted or attacked certain *mantravadis* or exorcists, who happened to pass through these hilly tracts.

The appearance of what is usually known as jack o'lantern on certain nights is looked upon with peculiar dread by the people of Malabar. These phantom lights are believed to be caused by light and fire sparks emitted from the mouths of peculiar devils who roam about the country. These devils make fishing their profession and livelihood. Like all of their kind they go out only in the night-time and particularly on rainy or foggy nights. They usually visit unfrequented localities, and the margins of tanks and other water-reservoirs. When they catch fish, they cook them by putting them in their mouths, which are but furnaces. They are said to disappear at the sight of human beings of whom they are in perpetual dread. It is curious to notice that they make their appearance only in marshy places and on foggy nights.

For the traditions connected with the goddess *Kali*, cholera and small-pox demons, *Vide* Chapter on "Some phases of religious life".

For the traditions connected with Mahabali *Vide* Chapter on the 'Onam Festival'; and *Vide* chapter on the 'Thiruvathira festival' for the traditions connected with the origin of Thiruvathira.

It is popularly believed that it is very unlucky to see the moon on a particular day in the year, called Chathurthi. Tradition says that this belief takes its origin from a curse pronounced on the moon by Ganapathi one of our mythical gods. This deity is usually represented in images as half man, half elephant and is stigmatised as a monstrous glutton whom no amount of food will satisfy. His abnormal gastric protuberance presents a very strange and hideous appearance. On one occasion, after a very sumptuous banquet, he was returning home in the clear moonlight. The effect of the grand feast was such that his stomach bulged out so much that he was unable to notice obstructions in the path. He was walking rather listlessly on account of the stupefying effect of his heavy meal. He came to a part of the path where there happened to be on either side brakes covered over with leaves and stalks which intertwined across the path. These the god did not perceive and at one point he slipped down and sustained some physical injury. He looked round to see if any one had noticed his fall. But none there was in sight except the moon above who, as soon as she saw the fall of the god, roared out laughing. This so irritated the god that he pronounced a curse on the moon to the effect that those who chanced to look at her on that particular night should fare very badly in society. Ugly scandals of diverse sorts would be spread against them, and they would be accused of theft, adultery and other heinous crimes. People to this day take every possible care to avoid seeing the moon or even her image in any reflecting medium on this particular night.

For the traditions connected with sorcery and witchcraft *vide* chapter on the 'Religious life.'

It is popularly supposed that by means of sorcery miracles can be worked if only men sufficiently skilled in the art can be found. But the belief is gradually losing ground and now finds an asylum only in the rustic imagination.

Eclipses also have a curious origin assigned to them in Malabar. Tradition says that when an eclipse takes place, Rahu, the huge serpent, is devouring the sun or the moon as the case may be. An eclipse being thus the decease of one of those heavenly bodies people must, of necessity, observe pollution for the period during which the eclipse lasts. When the monster spits out the body the eclipse is over. Food and drink taken during an eclipse possess poisonous properties, and people therefore religiously abstain from eating and drinking until the eclipse is over. They bathe at the end of the eclipse so as to get rid of the pollution. Any one shutting himself up from exposure may be exempted from this obligation to take a bath. The too frequent occurrence of eclipses forebodes the approach of calamities to the world.

An interesting origin is assigned to those sparks of fire which, on certain nights, are observed flying high up in the air. People believe in the existence inside the earth of a kind of precious stones called *Manikku Kallu*. These stones are supposed to have been made out of the gold which has existed in many parts of the earth from time immemorial. Certain serpents of divine nature have been blowing for ages on these treasures of gold, some of which under the process of blowing dwindle into a small tiny stone of resplendent beauty and brightness, which has obtained the appellation of *Manikka kallu*. The serpents work continuously without food or drink. The moment their work is finished they are transformed into winged serpents and fly up into the air with the stones lodged in their mouths. It is not known where these stones are carried to; but it is supposed that they are being taken to some vague and unknown land in the ethereal regions. There are traditions floating about in the land, which speak of men stricken with poverty, suddenly turning millionaires by coming into possession of one of these stones, which had fallen down owing to want of proper care on the part of the serpents.

In the case of some temples in the country Government has made large remissions of taxes. A somewhat humorous reason for these concessions has been given. It is said that the gods of the temples appeared unto the Collector of the district in warlike garb with bow strung, and arrows ready to shoot, and threatened to destroy him and the race he represented. These terrible phenomena necessitated the granting of remissions in taxation.

It is popularly believed that those who listen to the reading of the *Ramayana* lying on their beds are to be born blades of grass in the next birth. The crow and the barn-door fowl form the subject of a facetious myth. It is said that when these two animals were created they were separately questioned as to whether they desired personal beauty or long leases of life. The crow instantly indicated his desire for the latter, and hence he is believed to be the longest lived of the bird species. The fowl said that in his opinion it would be immensely better to be possessed of personal beauty than long life with an ugly and repulsive personal appearance. Hence the fowl is the shortest lived of birds.

The crow is believed to possess only one eye, though to all appearance, it has two separate eye-balls. This one ball is said to move first into one socket and then into the other as occasion demands. This myth has a very strange origin which dates as far back as the times of the Ramayana war. Rama, the hero of the epic, was banished into the jungles of Dandaka for fourteen years. His faithful wife Seetha accompanied him everywhere. Their staple food during their solitary peregrinations consisted of the flesh of wild animals which they took care to collect in large quantities for future consumption. The flesh was invariably dried in the sun so as to insure its preservation. On a certain occasion when flesh was thus exposed to the sun crows came and pecked at the ruddy fingers of Seetha's feet mistaking them for the blood-red pieces of flesh. Seetha, out of agony intimated the incident to Rama who had kept her on the watch for the purpose of scaring these troublesome creatures away. Rama took his bow and shot at them. An arrow entered the eye of one of the crows and destroyed it; and all his descendants have been blind of an eye. But Rama by a judicious exercise of his divine powers compensated the crow for this loss by enabling it to alter the position of the other eye ball as it desired. Hence all crows now share this characteristic peculiarity.

The three lines on the back of the squirrel are accounted for in a somewhat similar way. The story of their origin is as old as the legend of the blindness of the crow. Preliminary to the commencement of the Ramayana war, Rama was building the dam across the sea to Lanka, whither his wife had been carried by the wicked giant Ravana. In the work of building the dam animals of every class and species took part, and so the squirrel happened to be contributing its quota of work to the enterprise. Rama, on one occasion was supervising the work, when of all the animals engaged he noticed the squirrel. It was working rather very hard "with hunger gnawing at its vitals." The fatigued animal arrested his attention; and feeling pity for it he placed on its back the three middle fingers of his right hand; and after the customary fashion expressed his sympathy for it by gently drawing those fingers along its back. The impression left became the black and white lines which the entire species was thereafter to possess.

The hooting of the screech owl is said to forebode a death or a birth in the family nearest to the place where the noise is made. The exact nature of the event is thus recognized. If the cry comes from the southern quarter of the house it shows that a birth is shortly to take place in the house; if on the contrary, it comes from a northerly direction, then it is a death that is to be anticipated. The cries of the other two varieties of owls *viz.*, the snowy owl and the horned owl also forebode death. The crow, too, possesses prophetic power. Its cry is indicative of the arrival of guests from that quarter to which its tail is turned.

The cry of the bird called *Aripravu* (a kind of pigeons)

has a strange and pathetic history given to it. These birds are always found in pairs, the male and the female together. Once upon a time, the story goes, a pair of them were engaged in a game, when they quarrelled concerning some minor technical points connected with the game. The quarrel turned out so serious that the male deserted its mate; and ever after they remained separated. The female by and by found out the mistake which formed the basis of the quarrel; and when it cries it is said to be calling for its mate, its cry signifying that the mistake had been found out and that it can be rectified.

The monitor and the crocodile are held to belong to the same group of animals proceeding from the eggs of the crocodile. The eggs, when it is time for them to be hatched, burst open, and out of these spring forth number of little animals. Of the animals that come out some find their way into water, while others remain on the shore. The former become crocodiles and the latter monitors. Curious zoology indeed! The lizard is a great prophet of future events. There are experts who can tell the significance of its noise when made in particular ways and at particular periods of time or from particular directions. A fire fly getting inside a house at night is a sign that robbers will break into it that night.

The traditions connected with the origin of thunder, rain and lightning are no less amusing. In the regions above the earth there are supposed to exist huge monsters called

Kalameghathanmar to whom is assigned the responsibility of supplying the earth with water. These monsters are under the direction and control of Indra ; and are possessed of enormous physical strength. They have two huge horns projecting upwards from the sides of the crown of the head, large flashing eyes and other remarkable bodily features. All the summer they are engaged in drawing up water from the earth through their mouths, which they spit out to produce rain in the rainy season. A still ruder imagination ascribes rain to the periodical discharge of urine by these monsters. Hence in some quarters there exists a peculiar aversion to the use of rain water for ordinary human consumption. The monsters always work together, and in the process of working their huge horns sometimes come into violent collision with each other, producing a loud noise. This noise it is that is spoken of as thunder. The origin of lightning has however a more rational and scientific explanation given to it. The people have long had some idea of the production of fire by means of friction, and they say that lightning is caused by the friction of the horns of the monsters when engaged in their professional work. But some people attribute lightning to the flashes produced by the quick brandishing of Indra's sword in anger towards his rain-producing servants. However this may be, lightning-fire is an object of religious regard. It is believed to be "the divine fire," and is looked upon with mingled reverence and awe. People obtain this fire from trees that have been burnt by lightning; and they prèserve it as being as sacred as the fire of Vesta of the classical mythology.

There is a curious popular idea about the animals known as *Arana* and *Kuridi.* Tradition goes that when these animals were created, Arana was asked what it would do next after. The reply given was that it would bite any one it *thought* of biting or wished to bite. Hence the whole species was deprived of the power of *thinking.* Therefore the current idea is that the animal cannot think or concentrate its attention on any particular object; and that the moment it approaches any man for the purpose of biting him its thought is diverted from the man, its mind getting filled with other ideas; and it is thus obliged to leave him unmolested. Though these animals are perfectly harmless ones devoid of any poison inside, yet they are popularly believed to be so deadly poisonous that death is instantaneous in the case of a man bitten by them. (Cf. *Arana kadichal appol maranom* = If an Arana bites death is instantaneous.) Likewise the crawling animal *Kuridi.* This is believed to be a species of snakes of an eminently venomous character. Upon its being created it was also asked quite a similar question, *viz.*, what it would do. The prompt reply was that it would bite any one it *saw.* It was forthwith deprived of its eyesight and is still believed to be a blind creature incapable of *seeing* anything.

Another connected legend is that when the *Cobra* and

the *Arana* were created poison was supplied to them to be sucked from a leaf. The *Arana* took and sucked it wholesale leaving only the leaf smeared over with poison for the cobra to lap poison from; thereby implying that the cobra is far less venomous than the *Arana*; thus people greatly exaggerate the venomous character of the *Arana*.

The cobra is believed to be possessed of an infinite number of tiny legs with which it crawls along. It is said to subsist for days and days together upon the air it breathes.

The wood-pecker is spoken of as the bird carpenter. The night-moths are ants living inside the earth's entrails, which develop wings all of a sudden when rains begin to fall during the opening periods of the monsoons. The owls have no eyesight during day-time; but recover the same when darkness dawns. So also are the bats. There is a tradition which says that if anybody chances to mention the name of a lizard it cannot and will not find its prey for the day.

The earth is believed to be a flat body which is supported on the back of a huge monstrous fish or according to other beliefs on the back of a tortoise. Earthquakes are caused when the animal which forms the earth's support changes its position occasionally and thus causes the weight it supports to shake. The moon is a celestial body carrying on its bosom a hare or a rabbit which gets frightened by the rapid and threatening pursuit of the clouds. The stars are the spirits or souls of dead men which have become fixed high up in the heavens. When water is being boiled and evaporated it is believed to be drunk by the caldron or pot in which it is placed over the fire. The rainbow is the bow of Indra which he displays when the *kalameghathanmar* spoken of before cease drawing water from the earth.

The popular knowledge of geography is very meagre. Some people compress the whole created world into the one land of Malabar created by Parasu Rama; while others have a more extended knowledge of the subject because they have conceptions about Lunka of the Ramayana fame. In the former case Malabar is not merely what we now understand by the term but something more. The chameleon changes its color so very frequently because at the sight of human beings it attracts or draws to its own body the blood circulating in the body of the man that it keeps looking at. Hence it gets red in parts of its body.

The origins of certain classes of people are also of considerable importance in our national tales. The chief of those is the class generally known as the *Nambidis*. They are a class of regicide Brahmins who have, in consequence of the commission of sin, fallen away from the great trunk of Numbudri Brahmins. The tradition goes that the Numbudris became dissatisfied with the rule of their king Cheraman Perumal on account of his many acts of maladministration. They therefore resolved themselves into a social cabal and determined to murder him. This criminal and inhuman office was by common consent, assigned to one particular Nambudri. He promptly undertook the work, and proceeding against the king ruthlessly put an end to his life. After the deed was accomplished he came upon a company of Brahmins other than those implicated in the crime. By these he was offered a seat. But a keen sense of his heinous sin impelled him to decline the offer. He said he would be satisfied with a seat on the padi, (*a long piece of timber, cut and shaped and polished and permanently placed in the porticos of most Malayali houses to serve the purpose of a bench.*) This he expressed by the phrase *nam padi i.e.,* we shall be seated on this bench. This phrase *nam padi* was afterwards corrupted into *Nampadi* or *Nambidi.* The Brahmins found out why the Numbudri murderer declined the seat offered him and declaring him a murderer and a regicide they ostracised him from society and left him to take what course he would. He, having been thus socially outlawed, could not be admitted into any other caste. He was a married man himself and his wife naturally followed him. The sin of the first *Nambidi* was, like the inherited curse of Tantalus, visited upon all the succeeding generations of *Nambidis* who, to this day, form a peculiar class of Brahmins known by this distinctive appellation. There are likewise traditions connected with the origin of other classes of people, but none of them are so interesting as the tradition regarding the origin of the *Nambidis.*

There is a national understanding between the people of

north and south Malabar which to this day remains a standing blot upon the civilization of the country. The women of the country north of the Korapuzhe river, which is the geographical boundary between north and south Malabar, have social restrictions placed upon their free movements. They are not allowed, without prejudice to their social dignity, to cross that river and live in the southern parts. Those who do so are to this day looked upon as social outlaws. This restriction once existed among the southerners also, but is not now binding upon them. It is some consolation to know that the prohibition is confined to the female sex. Even women from the north now are discarding all scruples with regard to crossing over to the south, but not without opposition from the orthodox sects. It is said to have had its origin in the intestine feuds between the rulers of the north and the south in ancient times.

The Nambudri Brahmins of Malabar have all along been an inventive class; and their inventive genius has led them to the discovery of an important ethnological fact. This is nothing less than the origin of the English race. As is well-known, the war of the Ramayana was fought by armies of monkeys. At the conclusion of the war the remnants of the victorious army were gathered together in a large ship, to which a tremendously powerful push was given. The ship was, of course, destined for India; but owing to adverse circumstances on the way it did not reach India. It arrived at an unknown country far away, which was subsequently known by the name of *Blathi*, a corrupt form of *belal ethi* which means 'reached by force.' This *Blathi* is now identified with England. The monkey ship reached this land; and the crew disembarked and peopled it. Their descendants are the English people; and thus long before Darwin or Wallace ever dreamt of Evolution, the Numbudris of Malabar had a similar theory of the origin of at least a part of the human race.

The various superstitious beliefs which are cherished by the people are too many even to enumerate. They are common to all who profess the Hindu faith and are not peculiar to the Nairs. But as they are closely related to the religious thought of the people it will not be totally irrelevant in a treatise of this kind, which professes to deal with the Nair social life from various standpoints to mention a few of the many superstitions that corrupt the popular thought and reasoning. By the Nairs, as by all other Hindus, astrology is blindly believed in, and its predictions are closely followed and religiously acted upon. For every household ceremony auspicious days and auspicious moments have to be selected by means of astrology. This is done by men who are trained in the science. If any person, during the time that an eclipse lasts, happens to run a thorn into any part of his body that amounts to cobra-poisoning. The falling of an eclipse on a particular day is calamitous to any one whose birthday happens to coincide with the day of the eclipse; and to ward off the evils arising from the happening of an eclipse on one's birthday offerings of *pooja* and other thi ngs are made to the gods in the temples. Horoscopy is also blindly clung to. The Nairs are invariably believers in the dangerous doctrine of predestination; and their horoscopes pretend to reveal their future to them with infallible accuracy. Every decent Tarawad preserves the horoscope of every member. The first thing done immediately on the birth of a child is to ascertain the exact moment of its birth for which purpose clepsydras are invariably made use of. The child's horoscope is then constructed by professional astrologers, who predict from it the future of the child's life. A man's daily good-luck or ill-luck depends upon the nature of the first thing that he sees on opening his eyes after the previous night's sleep. If a man takes leave of a patient confined to bed, the man is likely to get the disease himself. Taking an oil bath and shaving on prohibited days bring disease, poverty and life-misfortunes upon the man so doing. Taking rice at nights on certain days, such as full moon days, carries similar consequences. The exact comparison of one thing with another tends to destroy or to prejudicially affect the thing with which the second object is compared. This is called *Karinkannidal.* During the pregnancy of any famale member of a Tarawad neither gold ornaments nor any vessels made of brass or bell-metal are to be given away or lent to a stranger for a whole day and night unless the man who takes them away gives in return for the things taken some metal of a similar kind. When a house is newly built the presumption is that one member of the family that built it must die. Itching of the palms of the hands and the soles of the feet forebodes the coming in of some money. Polluted things are purified by water prepared by Brahmins ; and in the worst cases of pollution what is called a *Panchagavyam* is resorted to. This is a mixture of five products of the sacred cow.

I do not pretend in the present chapter to have dealt with the subject in anything like an exhaustive manner. There are hundreds of traditions and superstitions yet remaining to be described. I have simply selected a few in order to illustrate certain features of the present stage of social life in Malabar. We are now in a state of transition. We are passing from a life unreasoning superstition to one of reason and enlightenment. With the diffusion of western thought in the country our social emancipation is being quickly accomplished. The ties of custom by which we have hitherto been bound down to the hoary traditions of our forefathers are gradually getting loosened. The superstitions and traditions of which I have written survive chiefly in the interior of the district. To the cultured mind nursed in the lap of modern science nymphs and fairies and demons are but monstrous unrealities. All

" The intelligible forms of ancient poets,
The fair humanities of old religion,
The power, the beauty, and the majesty.

That had their haunts in dale or piny mountain
Or forest by slow stream or pebbly spring
Or chasms and watery depths ; all these have vanished.
They live no longer in the faith of reason."

CHAPTER V.

THE MALABAR DRAMA.

Like all other Malabar institutions our drama is of the most primitive type. It assumes various forms of which Krishnattom and Ramanattom are the principal ones. The latter is usually called *Kadhakali* and constitutes our drama proper. I will now take these in order and explain their divers aspects.

But in tracing the genesis of our drama it is important to notice that it has originated from causes that have helped to produce the same amongst other nations and in other literatures. Just as the "*Mysteries*" or *Miracle Plays* which expound in living embodiments of human characters the sacred incidents of the Bible, and after them what are known as the *Moralities* have been the germ out of which the subsequent dramatic literature of Europe has developed, our drama has similarly arisen from our desire to exhibit in living shapes the holy stories of our Puranas of which the central figures are Rama and Krishna, both incarnations of Vishnu. This will be noticed from the following accounts of it, collected from the living traditions current amongst us.

Krishnattam.—Its origin is lost in antiquity. There are traditions current which ascribe that origin to one of the old

Zamorins of Calicut. One pious devotee of Sri Krishna, by name Villuvamangalth Swamiar took his residence close by Krishna in his famous temple at Guruvayur in the suburbs of Chowghaut, offering prayers and leading a most religious and saintly life. The Zamorins of those days were reigning princes; and the temple at Guruvayur was therefore within their territorial jurisdiction. One of these sovereigns in those by gone days started on a pilgrimage to this temple. After some days of stay in the place, the king being himself a pious man besought the Swamiar to find him an opportunity of personally witnessing the divine figure. The request was granted and the king was asked to be present one night at a particular spot in the temple, where Krishna was accustomed to be engaged in his boyish pastimes. The king appeared there at the appointed hour and saw the god in all the fresh splendour of his puerile divinity. And being fondly enamoured of the boy-god he could not restrain himself and there he ran up to him and caught him by the head. Krishna thereupon hurriedly disappeared and in the confusion of the moment the king was able to pluck a single peacock-feather from his head-dress. This the king preserved and from that time was seized with the idea of using it on Krishna's head-dress and dramatising the Puranic incidents connected with him. The king was himself a man of profound scholarship in Sanskrit and of splendid poetical talents. He thereafter betook himself to the task of composing in Sanskrit a drama in commemoration of the deeds and life of Krishna. The scheme was matured in a few years and the drama was completed, the life-history of Krishna being the main thread on which the narrative was constructed.

Such is the origin of Krishnattom, which occupies a conspicuous place in the dramatic literature of our country. This drama, unlike the other one, is of a peculiar kind. The characters who appear on the stage indulge in no significant gesture language. The movements of the hands made by the actors are not suggestive of any special meaning. The full drama is sufficient for eight days' acting, beginning with the birth of Krishna and ending with his lamented death. On the ninth day, the birth-scene is again enacted, the reason being the instinctive popular aversion for leaving the god in his last moments. Only places of sanctity and purity are fit for the performance. The descriptions of the various elements that constitute the other kind of drama will mostly fit in with *Krishnattam* also except that in the latter, the duration for the acting is theoretically a little over three hours commencing about 10 and closing at about 1 or 1-30, in the evening. It is not to be performed anywhere and everywhere, but only in certain particularized places sanctioned by the Zamorin. The charge for a day's performance exclusive of the feeding of the actors, &c., is 64 fanams equivalent to Rs. 18-4-7.

The other kind of drama is what is called *Kdhakali*,

formerly known as *Ramanattam*. This celebrates the deeds and history of Rama, another of Vishnu's incarnations. It apparently possesses a secular origin; but one grounded upon the desire to celebrate the story of Rama.

This origin is related thus. On one occasion the Raja of Kottayam sent an embassy to the Zamorin requesting him to send over his *Krishnattam* drama to his palace at Kottayam. The request was indignantly refused, and the Kottayam Raja being himself a Sanskrit scholar and poet composed the first four pieces in succession such as *Kalyanasougandhikam*, *Baka Vadham*, *Kalakeya Vadham*, and *Krimeera Vadham* which form practically the nucleus about which has gathered the subsequent dramatic literature of our country. Later on, other writers followed suit and in the space of a few years the number of dramas swelled to fifty-six. Even now the process of dramatic development in our land is not complete. Each subsequent writer gifted with poetical talents contributes his mite; and at the present day the total number cannot be far behind seventy.

Before describing in detail the other aspects of this variety of drama, I will first give a brief account of a day's performance.

The actors all generally go about from house to house and arrange for the performance. A particular house is first selected and at about 5-30 or so in the evening what is called the *Keli kayyu* begins, with the systematic but mingled beat of drums *Elathalam* and *Chengala* (two other instruments described later on). This is to herald aloud the intended performance of the drama on that particular night. About 6 P. M. the actors begin to paint their faces. About 8 or 8-30 the lamp is lighted. Only one lamp is used on the occasion. Then what is known as *Thodayam* commences. This consists of songs and the initiation of little boys into the mysteries of stage-performance, with drum-beating &c. all carried on inside the curtain. Next the *Vandana slogam viz.*, some song in praise of some god is sung. After this follows the *Purapad* or the appearance of the first character. The most important one appears first usually, attended with great stir and confusion occasioned by the loud and bold beatings of drums and extra torch lights held in hand on both sides of the actor, by two others. But this character appears not at the beginning always but only at his appointed place in the play. The interval between the *Purapad* and the regular appearance of characters is filled up with *Melappadam i.e.*, songs, drum-beating &c., but without any curtain being hung. Immediately after this, begins the regular appearance of the characters of the play.

Such characters may be divided into *Pacha, Kathi, Thadi* (red, black and white) *Kari, Minukku Veshom, Veesa Ezhuthu* and the *female characters*. There are likewise some others also such as those with white spots on the actor's face already painted red, and the painting of a clown which is, at best, a curious mixture of every incongruous and absurd element of painting.

I will now proceed to give a descriptive account of these various types of characters of our drama.

1. *Pacha.* (Green painting). The face is painted over with *manola* (a green mixture in certain definite proportions of sulphur and another substance in cocoanut oil). The edges of the eyelids and also the eyebrows are likewise painted with black soot mixed with oil or ghee. Then a small coating of *chotti* is made with a mixture of chunam and rice-flour along the chin and the cheek-bones. The chief characters who appear in Pacha are the five members of the *Pandava* sect, *Indra*, *Nalan*, the famous king, *Pushkara* his antagonist, *Krishna*, also the King of the *Virada* country, and *Rama*, *Lakshmana* and a few others.

2. *Kathi.*—First the face is painted green with *manola* and in the middle a red painting of a peculiar twist and twin called a *Kathi* is made. Outside this and along the borders comes a painting of black. Then again outside this *manola* is painted along symmetrically with the black painting. Next what is called a *chotti* which is a thick coating with an uneven, wavelike surface made of a combination of chunam and rice-flour, is drawn along. Both these kinds of characters wear crowns made of stones, glass, beetle-shells, silverknobs, blanket, and gilded metal leaf all arranged in set and orderly forms and called *Kesabharam kireetam.* The principal characters of this type are *Ravana*, the famous Rakshasa king, *Keechakan*, *Narakasuran*, *Krimeeran*, and a few others.

3. *Thadi* (beard).—This assumes three distinct varieties, such as red, white and black, according as the beard put on is made of materials of one or the other of these colors.

The red is named *Chukanna Thadi.* The crown put on is called *Kuttichamaram* and is made of the materials mentioned before. But in this case, the frame is made of wood, with red hangings of thread on the borders. The face is painted with a *red* coating. Then a black line with a curl and turn is drawn. Then small flower-shaped substances made of the *Kedesu* plant or cork are stuck on. Then a rounded knob made of the same plant is stuck on the tip of the nose and another on the forehead which is permanently attached to a long piece of cloth tied round the head along the forehead. In the case of some characters the number of knobs on the forehead is three. A *red* beard of artificial construction is also worn. A *red* coat is worn on the person. The chief characters of this description are *Bali*, *Sugreevan*, and *Angadan* who are monkeys, *Kalakeyan*, *Jerasandhan*, *Narakasuran*, the major, and a few others, with slight deviations from the established methods of face-painting and adorning. Amongst Rakshasas all reigning kings may have *Kathi* and all others, *Thadi*.

The *white one* is called *Vellathadi*. In this case also first comes the red painting on the face. Then on it one of black soot mixed with some oily substance. A long *white* artificial beard is worn, as also a *chotti* as before described. A *white* coat with white hangings all over is worn on the person. A knob in the middle of the forehead and the tip of the nose is also put on. *Hanuman*, *Vividen Nandikesaran* all belong to this type of characters. Then inferior monkeys are of various forms with different monkey-faces.

The Black one is styled the *Karuthathadi*. A black painting is given to the face and also a red one. Then a *Chotti* as described before is made along the chin and cheek-bones; also flower-shaped substances made of cork materials are stuck thereon. But there are some without this item. A *black* artificial beard is worn together with a black head-dress. The coat worn is made of *black* tinted cloth but without the hangings as in the case of the red and white *Thadis*. In the case of all *Thadis*, the eyes are painted black. *Kuttalan*, *Kali* and *Neelan* are the chief of this variety.

4. *Kari.*—The face is colored with a black plaint and on each of the two cheeks a crescent-shaped drawing is inscribed. On the forehead is put a mark made of white manola and red paint. The edges of the eyelids and also the eyebrows are painted white with white manola and *Chotti* is also drawn. A *black* dress, *black* coat and long breasts and two large prominent artificial dog-teeth are put on. This is common to all *Thadis* likewise. The dress down the waist is a folded one with black cloth; and small branches of trees or plants held in hand together complete the habiliment of this type of characters.

5. *Minikku Veshams*, have a head-dress tapering upwards and ending in a bunch or knob. The face is smeared over with

white *manola* paint. The eyes and eyebrows are painted black. A long magnificent white beard is worn. A piece of printed cloth is also put on round the waist. There is no coat used, but there are brummagem jewellery used. Brahmins and all Rishis belong to this class.

6. *Veesa Ezhuthu.*—The face is painted with white manola and the eyes, and eyebrows and beard are also coated with a black paint. In this case the beard is only drawn with a paint and no artificial beard is utilized. All carpenters and *Madolghadan* are of this type.

7. *Female* characters differ in different dramas; but all of them appear in female dress.

The dress from down the waist is the same for all *Theppu Veshams, viz.*, trousers and printed cloths. Long silver nails are worn on the fingers by all except female characters.

A singular variety in our dramatic performances consists in what is styled a *Nanam.* In some plays there are incidents dramatized which relate to some most inhuman and unchivalrous acts such as chopping off the breasts and nose of females, committed by persons of position and influence. In such cases the plays merely make mention of such cruel deeds; and ordinarily they are represented on the stage only in theory and the whole thing is allowed to pass off smoothly. But on particular occasions, if people are so minded, they arrange for this *Nanam* in which the actor representing the poor, victimized woman is dressed up in a nose and breasts such as could easily be chopped off; so that the actual deed is in practice represented on the stage. This is done in the following manner. A large quantity of rice-flour and turmeric powder are mixed and boiled and completely reddened with the addition of chunnam. This is mixed up with the flowers of the areca-branch. Then a long chain is made of tender cocoanut-leaves so as to resemble the human intestines and is enveloped in a piece of cloth. Then a pair of human breasts are made of the bark or film of the areca-branch and are attached to the chest of the actor. On this the said artificial chain is left hanging. An artificial nose is then made of the same substance and is placed on the nose of the actor, and on this, pieces of rags are also suspended. The leaf-chain, and breasts and nose are all dipped in the red liquid mixture and are given an appearance of blood-smearing. These are worn on the person of the actor who is already smeared all over with the red mixture. Thus he is given an air such as would indicate the actual and physical commission of some terrific process of mutilation on his person. The actor appears on the stage from the front side with big torch-lights on both sides held in hand by two men, and supported by two others who help him from imminent prostration on the ground. The whole scene is an extremely interesting one; though its terror-striking appearance would seem, for a time, to mar the mirth and solemnity of the occasion. The scene closes and additional presents are given to this actor for all his troubles, at the close of the performance.

The Malabar drama is an itinerant institution carried on by a number of persons. The *lamps* used on the occasions are constructed purely after native fashion out of bell-metal materials. It is filled with oil and a number of big torches made of old torn cotton cloths tightly rolled up and dipped in oil are lighted and placed in it thus giving increased light. This is to be furnished by those who get the acting done. The *curtain* is usually some large and thick piece of cloth or pieces stitched together into one large cloth, inscribed with the figures of some animals or gods or the like. On two ends of this cloth two small but heavy balls of cloth are left hanging. These are held on the stage by two men at the commencement of the drama as well as on the appearance of every character. Another square curtain with hangings on the borders is suspended horizontally from over the heads of the actors on the appearance of every important character. Sometimes conch-shells are blown in order to increase the solemnity of the occasion. The *seats* used on the stage by the actors consist of mortars turned upside down; and forest scenes are represented by big branches of trees stuck on the ground near the stage. The *stage* is not, as in European dramas, as raised platform or dais; but the bare ground in front of the spectators cleared and wetted with water or dug up and beaten down so as to prevent dust from flying about to the nuisance of the spectators. The latter seat themselves on the ground and on mats they themselves bring with them; and sometimes chairs and other seats are supplied by the house-owner, but not generally. The main *instruments* of the drama are drums of two kinds; one beaten with the fingers of the hands and called a *Muddalum* and the other beaten with drum-sticks and called a *Chenda*. The former are of two kinds; the large one and the small one. *Chengala* is another of these instruments. It is a small thick circular instrument with one surface slightly bulging out and made of bell-metal, to which a small cord is attached through two holes drilled near the circumference. This is held on the thumb of the left hand by the cord tied together; and the convex surface is struck in a certain rhythmic order with a small stick held in the right hand. There is also another instrument called an *Elathalam* which consists of two small thick circular pieces of bell-metal instruments each with a protrusion in the middle to each of which is attached a small strong cord through a hole bored in that middle portion. Each of these is held by the cord in each of the hands and the two are forcefully struck against each other in a certain well-defined order. These instruments and the drums are so beaten as to produce a ringing rhythmic sound fitting in with the music of the singers. A senior singer called *Ponnani* and a junior one called a *Sankidi* do all the singing business. There are invariably five boxes of deal-wood set apart for particular items of the paraphernalia of the drama; such as an·

1. *Uduthukettupetti*, for keeping all the dress from the waist downwards.

2. *Kireetapetti*, for keeping the head-dress.

3. *Koppupetti*, for dress, ornaments &c.

4. *Vellipetti*, for the silver ornaments.

5. *Chandipetti*, for miscellaneous articles such as the various paints &c.

The drums &c. are all tied up into one big bundle.

The least number of persons required for a performance is 30 including 12 actors 4 singers both junior and senior, 4 drummers of the two kinds of drums, two chottikkars or men whose function is to paint the chotti described before, and 6 box-carriers, 1 washerman and a Brahmin to serve as a cook. There are also some weapons and instruments in requisition; such as a wooden instrument called a *Chakkram*, swords, clubs, bows and arrows also a plough in some cases, a conch-shell, a curtain, an *Alavattam* or a kind of circular instrument with peacock feathers stuck on the circumference and some other common embellishments on a frame, with a wooden handle. Different varieties of faces are also to be in store to exhibit different kinds of faces.

In some plays what is called a *Poli* is instituted by those at whose expense the play is acted. In the middle of a performance about midnight or so the performance is suspended for a while and the poli begins; which consists in sums of money subscribed by the invited section of the spectators. This money goes to those who get the play acted on the particular night. On such occasions some one of the actors dresses himself in a clown's attire, makes his appearance on the stage and intensely amuses the audience with his jokes and funs. He receives a present of a few annas, usually four and goes his own way. On rare occasions when some specialist actor displays his special skill in the performance, some of the spectators make extra presents to him in the shape of money or grand clothes and for still more extraordinary display of dramatic skill what we know of as a *Veera-srinkala*, a golden bracelet of a chain-shaped pattern with a fastening in one place and having a few rupees' weight. The usual charge for a day's performance is Rs. 10, and meals for the day for all engaged in the drama. The cost of the materials of a drama is about Rs. 400. The plays are generally acted inside a temporary small square shed made with four poles stuck on the ground at equal distances on which small bamboo beams are arranged. The roof is covered with thatchings made of cocoanut-leaves. The four sides are left open.

Our drama is altogether a dumb-show in which the actors never utter a word but do everything by signs and gestures. All the music is done by the singers. The actors come on the stage silently and indulge in significant gestures corresponding to the subject-matter of the part sung. There are altogether sixty-four of these gestures to express human ideas; and any deficiency is made up by combinations of these sixty-four gestures. In some parts of the play the gestures are to be accompanied with significant facial distortions which require great skill and cleverness. Changes of thought and feeling such as anger, sorrow, joy &c., in the minds of persons represented by particular actors should be exhibited by the latter so every naturally and unaffectedly as to be considered actual changes taking place in the minds of such persons whom the actors represent. Herein consists most of the skill and expertness of the actors. The high caste people of Malabar have from their cradle been taught to believe in the sacred genuineness of the Puranic incidents ; and those who act the part of those old worthies of our Puranas are held in great admiration and respect by these zealots. It is agreeably pleasant to observe certain zealous admirers of these dumb-shows gazing in rapturous admiration at the skill and cleverness of some specialist actor who has acquired renown in the dramatic art. They would fain forego every worldly blessing for the enjoyment of its æsthetic pleasures.

Our dumb-show, from our national standpoint, embraces almost all that would please the human senses. The fond musician with his special gifts of musical talents can cheerfully enjoy the pleasures of our native airs with their

> " Many a winding bout
> Of linkèd sweetness long drawn out."

The rough drummer can delightfully revel in the pauses and rhythm of drum-beating. The expert in gesture language sees in the gestures of the specialist actor that inherent element of pleasure and of amusement which it requires his special eye to detect and his special mind to enjoy. He can inwardly perceive and feel the close natural resemblance between the feigned exhibition of the diverse feelings on the stage by such actor and the actual birth of impulses in the breast of him whom he represents in the play. The untutored boor, who though unable to understand and appreciate the significance of the acting and enjoy the pleasures attending it, is nevertheless stirred up into energy on the appearance of some ferocious characters whose loud cries and stentorian depth of voice are heard at great distances and distinct from the deafening beat of drums, music and other accompaniments of the drama. But all the same our drama requires to be purged of those obscene elements which, by popular suffrage and the sanction of ages, are still retained in the form of kissing and embracing by the characters on the public stage where figure amongst the spectators the modest forms of the fair sex. And we fervently hope that this defect which is perceivable only when looked at through the glasses of modern refinement will soon be remedied and removed and the old and interesting institution preserved in a new, refined and purified form.

CHAPTER VI.

THE ONAM FESTIVAL.

This important Malabar Festival is in commemoration of the reign of Mahabali which is believed to have been one uninterrupted period of peace, plenty and prosperity; and in fact the golden age of our national history. Theft, robbery, murder and other crimes were altogether unknown as may be seen from the following couplet:

> " Maveli nadathu vazhum kalam
> Kalla kkedilla kalavu milla,"

which may be freely translated as follows:

> " When Mahabali ruled the land
> There was no theft nor dread of thiefs."

The national calm that prevailed was not disturbed by any acts of cruelty or oppression. The sanctity of contracts was fully realized. Honesty of purpose and probity of character were the dominant guides to every man's actions. In short men in those days lived in what has been called " a state of nature." This reign of nature was brought to a close by Vamana, the fifth incarnation of Vishnu, one of the members of our Divine Trinity. Mahabali was an Asura king against whom and whose prosperous reign the Devas entertained the deepest class-hatred and jealousy. With the object of putting an end to Mahabali's reign, the Devas repaired to Vishnu's presence and importuned him to adopt some means to cripple the increasing prosperity of Mahabali. Vishnu readily acceded to the request and appeared as Vamana unto the king in all "the glory and freshness of his youth." The king was so madly enamoured of this "gilded youth" that he resolved to welcome him at any cost. He asked the youth what he wanted; to which the boy replied that he wanted nothing more than three feet of earth. The demand was at once conceded; when the boy immediately assumed a gigantic figure and with his huge feet began to measure the earth. It was then found that the whole of the land measured less than three feet; and for the rest of the proferred earth Vamana trod upon Mahabali's head and pushed him down to the infernal regions. But the popular outcry consequent upon Mahabali's deposition was so great that the ex-ruler was eventually allowed to return to the earth once a year. The period of his visit was fixed for the Malayalam month of Chingam corresponding to about August or September; and his stay in the country, short though it is, has ever since been celebrated as a grand national occasion which is now identified with the Onam Festivals. It is said that during the reign of Mahabali the whole year round was marked by pomp and revelry such as prevail during the short period of the Onam. And the Onam festival forms the period during which Mahabali is supposed to re-visit the earth to see how the country prospers in his absence.

The festival lasts according to local variations for four, five or six days during which time feasting and games, mirth and jollity prevail. It concerns chiefly the male members, although females also, as a matter of course, enjoy the pleasantry and merry-making. The festival opens practically ten days before the Thiruvonam day when every family makes a point of beginning to keep the houses extra clean. A portion of the yard around the house and inside it is cleansed every morning with cow-dung water and elegantly beautified with the figures of certain birds, and animals made of flowers of varied colors strewn carefully in peculiar artistic fashions; so that the mornings look exceedingly bright and cheerful. On the opening day there is a small element of festivity universally indulged in. In some places the Onam begins two or three days before the Thiruvonum day. But strictly speaking it commences only on the Thiruvonum day. The opening of the festival is marked by the distribution of clothes in the shape of presents by the heads of every respectable Tarawad to the juniors and immediate relatives as well as to servants and workmen. The junior members also sometimes give presents to their relatives and hangers-on; but not to such an extent as in the case of Karanavans or heads of families. The people enjoy the merriment and revelry. They go about in the finest attire and in the neatest possible fashion. Images made of sticky clay of peculiar shapes with flower-branches stuck on the tops, are fashioned and kept in prominent places which are decorated with lines tastefully drawn along and about with water mixed with rice-flour and sanctified with a coating of cow-dung water, both inside and outside the house; and offerings of pooja are made to them both morning and evening by some one before the inmates begin to take their meals. This continues right up to the close of the festival. These images are called *Thrikka Karuppan*; and they are introduced into the house on the day previous to the Thiruvonam day. After the dedication of these images a concourse of people band themselves together and raise a peculiar rhythmic shouting cry; which practically proclaims the approach of Onam. The feasting all along is on a very grand scale; the essential element in it is Ninthrapazhom or *benana*, a plantain fruit almost indigenous to Malabar. They are taken and cut in twos and threes, and boiled in water and are eaten along with the various meals; the intervals between which also being sometimes closed up by fresh editions of plantain-eating. Both male and female members of the family sit together apart at meals. By midday the principal meal is over and then each one goes his own way to participate in the out-door merry-making. Field games such as foot-ball matches, personal combats, games of chess, dice and cards, and dancing by females and music parties constitute the leading enjoyment from morning till evening. Foot-ball matches are different in detail to the corresponding European ones. A small stick is planted at a fixed spot, and people especially young lusty men resolve themselves into two rival camps and open the match. One party stands at the post, while the other stands a little away from it. The ball which is usually made of coir rope is propelled amain with the palm of the hand towards the rival party who furiously scramble for it vying with each other to catch it and stop its onward career. This done, one of the members takes it in hand and aiming at the post throws the ball in its direction. If the ball hits the post or if any one member of the hostile rank catches the ball in its progress up through the air, but not when it has once touched the ground, then that particular player's turn is over. Then another man takes up the play and continues it; and when all the members of the one party have had each his turn then the rival section begins the play exactly in the same manner and under the same rules as the previous section. The process is continued time after time and then the whole lot of them together declare the issue of the match.

Combats are of two kinds, viz., those that are undertaken singly and those held in batches. In the first the people of one locality divide themselves into two batches. When the match is opened the leader of one group sends forth one trained pugilist who paces along the intervening stretch of ground between the two groups shaking hands and challenging to meet in fair combat any one from the opposite camp. A little while after some one from the other party takes up the gauntlet and then after a few preliminary manœuvres the combat is begun. Every privilege and facility of a fair nature is afforded to the two combatants. The issue of the fight is watched with eager concern by all interested spectators and the successful man is then deluged with presents of money and clothes by the rich and generous amongst the members. This process is then continued for sometime till the close of the day. The next kind goes by the name of *Attakalam*. This is essentially a boyish pastime though grown men also at times take part in it. A large circle is drawn on the plain sand floor and people are selected for each of the two sections from amongst the assemblage. One section is then placed in a collective body inside the circle, while the other stands around the outside. The latter then try, with of course as little personal injury to themselves as possible, to strike at and bring outside, the former who are inside, each by each. In the interval between one outsider getting inside and touching the body of any one amongst the inside group the latter are allowed to beat and worry the antagonist. But the moment he touches the person of the inside man he obtains complete immunity from violence at the hands of the rest of the inside batch. But the person who is caught is at liberty to strike him and struggle to prevent his being driven out. If he gets turned out then he is no more to remain inside; and when the whole of the inside section are thus driven out, the first batch has finished its turn and is then followed up by the other batch; and if any body is left inside who cannot be driven out, his party is declared successful. Sometimes presents are given to the winners as tokens of appreciation of their training and strength.

A kind of peculiar bow formed of a strong and slightly elastic wood with a small cord made of bamboo materials and attached to both ends of the bow by means of two knobs, which when played on by means of a small stick produces a very dulcet musical tone is the familiar plaything for children. Sometimes they join together and organize a sort of bow-party ; and the pastime interests them deeply.

The only other prominent item of enjoyment is dancing by young maidens. A number of these join together in a circular row at a pre-arranged spot and begin the dancing. The airs are many and varied. Some of them are isolated ones composed in pure Malayalam touching some specialized topic ; while there are some other and more dignified ones extracted from the dramatic literature of the country. Now standing in a ring without touching each other one member thereof opens the ball by reciting one couplet from one of these songs. She is then caught up by others in equally melodious and profuse strains. Then she sings the next couplet and is then followed up by the rest of the party collectively and so on until the whole song is exhausted. Then another girl begins with another song which is similarly ended and so on the process goes. Thus the whole surrounding atmosphere of many a leading household is filled by the vociferous yet dulcet melody of charming choirs of lady singers adding to the jollity and attractiveness of the occasion all round.

Thus closes the Onam festival. On the last day the aforesaid clayey images are removed in the evening for which an auspicious day is selected, and the removal is symbolized by rhythmic shouting similar to that which marked it at the inauguration. The close of the festival is awaited with anxious solicitude by the people who when taking away these images on the closing day do so with special requests to them to come back again the next year.

Then there is the tail-end of the Onam called *Pathinaram makam*. It comes off exactly on the sixteenth day from the Thiruvonam day when also the festivities of the Onam are indulged in to much the same extent as before.

CHAPTER VII.

THE VISHU FESTIVAL.

Vishu, like the Onam and the Thiruvathira Festivals, is a remarkable event amongst us. Its duration is limited to one day. The 1st of Medom (some day in April) is the unchangeable day on which it falls. Its origin is almost hopelessly obscured by time. It is practically the Astronomical New Year's Day and has many aspects in common with what is known as the *Hoolie*. This was one of the periods when in olden days the subjects of ruling princes or authorities in Malabar under whom their lots were cast, were expected to bring their New Year's offerings to such princes. Failure to comply with the said customary and time-consecrated demands was visited with royal displeasure resulting in manifold varieties of oppression. The British Government finding this was a great burden pressing rather heavily upon the people, obtained as far back as 1790, a binding promise from those Native Princes that such exactions of presents from the people should be discontinued thereafter. Consequently it is now shorn of much of its ancient sanctity and splendour. But suggestive survivals of the same are still to be found in the presents (explained further on) which tenants and dependants bring to leading families on the day previous to the Vishu, called Sankramam, and in some places on the morning of the Vishu day. But such presents are no longer compulsory in nature, but only permissive with no enforceable penalty attaching to them.

Being thus the commencement of a New Year, native superstition surrounds it with a peculiar solemn importance. It is believed that a man's whole prosperity in life depends upon the nature, auspicious or otherwise, of the first things that he happens to fix his eyes upon on this particular morning. According to Nair and even general Hindu Mythology there are certain objects which possess an inherent inauspicious character. For instance ashes, firewood, oil and a lot of similar objects are inauspicious ones which will render him who chances to notice them first fare badly in life for the whole year, and their obnoxious effects will be removed only on his seeing holy things, such as, reigning princes, oxen, cows, gold and such-like ones on the morning of the next New Year. Whereas wholesome and favourable consequences can be produced by the sight of auspicious objects like those just enumerated. The effects of the sight of these various materials are said to apply even to the attainment of objects by a man starting on a special errand who happens for the first time to look at them after starting. However, with this view, almost every family religiously takes care to prepare the most sight-worthy objects on the New Year morning. Therefore, on the previous night they prepare what is known, in native phraseology, as a *kani*. A small circular bell-metal vessel is taken and some holy objects are systematically arranged inside it. A Grandha or old book made of palmyra leaves, a gold ornament, a new-washed clothe, some "unprofitably gay" flowers of the *Konna* tree, a measure of rice, a so-called looking-glass made of bell-metal, and a few other things, are all tastefully arranged in the vessel and placed in a prominent room inside the house. On either side of this vessel two brass or bell-metal lamps filled with cocoanut oil "clear as diamond sparks" are kept intensely burning and a small plank of wood or some other seat is placed in front of it. At about 5 o'clock in the morning of the day some one who has got up first wakes up the inmates, both male and female, of the house and takes them blindfolded so that they may not gaze at anything else, to the seat near the Kani. The members are seated one after another in the seat and are then and not till then asked to open their eyes and carefully look at this Kani. Then each is made to look at some venerable, old grey-haired member of the house or sometimes a stranger even. This over, the little playful urchins of the house begin to fire small crackers which they have bought and stored for the occasion. The Kani is then taken round the place from house to house for the benefit of the poor families, which cannot afford to prepare such a costly adornment. With the close of the carelessly confused noise of the crackers the morning breaks and preparations are begun for the morning meal. This meal is in some parts confined to rice-kanji with a grand appendage of other eatable substances and in others to ordinary rice and its accompaniments, but in either case on grand scales.

Immediately the day dawns the heads of the families give to almost all the junior members and servants of the household and to wives and children, money-presents varying from 4 as. to a rupee or two. Children preserve these presents to serve as their pocket money. In the more numerically large families similar presents are also made by the heads of particular branches of the same family to their juniors, children, wives and servants. These presents are intended to be the forerunners of incomes to them more splendid all the year round.

But one other item connected with the festival deserves mention. On the evening of the previous day, about four or five o'clock most well-to-do families distribute paddy or rice, as the case may be, in varying quantities with some other accessories to the family-workmen, whether they live on the family-estates or not. In return for this these labourers bring with them for presentation the fruits of their own labours such as vegetables of divers sorts, cocoanut oil, jaggery, plantains, pumpkins, cucumbers, brinjals &c., in ways such as their respective circumstances might permit.

With the close of the noon-meal the festival practically concludes, and nothing remains of it for the next day or for the same evening, for that matter. In some families after the noon-meals are over, dancing and games of various kinds are carried on, which contribute to the enhancement of the pleasantries incidental to the festival. As on other prominent occasions, card-playing and other games are also resorted to. However, these enjoyments are only of an ephemeral character lasting for only a few hours or at most a day.

CHAPTER VIII.

THE THIRUVATHIRA FESTIVAL.

Thiruvathira is one of the three great national occasions of Malabar. It generally comes off in the Malayalam month of Dhanu (December or January) on the day called the Thiruvathira day. It is essentially a festival in which females are almost exclusively concerned and lasts for but a single day. It has got behind it a traditional antiquity stretching back to times almost out of mind. The popular conception of it is that it is in commemoration of the death of Kamadevan, the Cupid of our national mythology. As recorded in the old Puranas, Kamadevan was destroyed in the burning fire of the third eye of Siva, one of the chief members of our Divine Trinity. Hence he is now supposed as having only an ideal or rather spiritual existence, and thus he exerts a powerful influence upon the lower passions of human nature. The memory of this unhappy tragedy is still kept alive amongst us, particularly the female section, by means of the annual celebration of this important festival. About a week before the day, the festival practically opens. At about 4 in the morning every young female member of Nair families with pretensions to decency, gets out of her bed and takes her bath in a tank. Usually, a fairly large number of these young ladies collect themselves in the tank for the purpose.

Then all or almost all of these plunge in the water and begin to take part in the singing that is presently to follow. One of these then leads off by means of a peculiar rhythmic song chiefly pertaining to Cupid. This singing is simultaneously accompanied by a curious sound produced with her hand on the water. The palm of the left hand is closed and kept immediately underneath the surface of the water. Then the palm of the other is forcibly brought down in a slanting direction and struck against its surface. So that the water is completely ruffled and is splashed in all directions producing a loud deep noise. This process is continuously prolonged together with the singing. One stanza is now over along with the sound and then the leader stops awhile for the others to follow her in her wake. This being likewise over, she caps her first stanza, with another at the same time beating on the water and so on until the conclusion of the song. Then all of them make a long pause and then begin another. The process goes on until the peep of dawn when they rub themselves dry and come home to dress themselves in the neatest and grandest possible attire. They also darken the fringes of their eyelids with a sticky preparation of soot mixed up with a little oil or ghee; and sometimes with a superficial coating of antimony powder. They also wear white, black, or red marks lower down the middle of their foreheads close to the part where the two eyebrows near one another. They also chew betel and thus redden their mouths and lips. Then they proceed to the enjoyment of another prominent item of pleasure *viz.*, swinging to and fro, on what is usually known as an Uzhinjal. A long bamboo piece is taken and rent asunder from the root end of it leaving the other end whole and untouched. Then two holes are bored, one on the cut end of each one of the two parts into which the bamboo is split. Now another but a small piece of the same material about a yard in length is divided along the grain into two equal parts. One of these is taken and its both ends are cut into points which are thrust into the two holes of the long bamboo pieces spoken of before. This is securely nailed and strongly attached to the long bamboo; which is then hung by means of a very tight strong rope to a strong horizontal branch of a neighbouring tree. Then the player seats herself on the small piece attached between the split portions which are firmly held by her two hands; and then the whole thing is propelled amain by some one from behind. These ladies especially derive immense pleasure from this process of swinging backwards and forwards, sometimes very wide apart so as to reach the other and higher branches of the tree. Nevertheless, accidents are few and far between. This as well as the songs and early bath all close on the festival day when still greater care and scrupulousness are bestowed upon the various elements of enjoyments.

On the festival day after the morning bath is over, they take a light chota and in the noon the family-dinner is voraciously attacked; the essential and almost universal ingredients of which being ordinary ripe plantain fruits and a delicious perparation of arrow-root powder purified and mixed with jaggery or sugar and also cocoanut. Then till evening dancing and merry-making are ceaselessly indulged in.

The husband population are inexcusably required to be present in the wives' houses before evening as they are bound to do on the Onam and Vishu occasions; failure to do which is looked upon as a step or rather the first step on the part of the defaulting husband towards a final separation or divorce from the wife. Despite the rigour of the bleak December season during which commonly the festival falls, heightened inevitably by the constant blowing of the cold east wind upon their moistened frames, these lusty maidens derive considerable pleasure from their early baths and their frolics in water. The biting cold of the season which makes their persons shiver and quiver like aspen-leaves before the breeze, becomes to them in the midst of all their ecstatic frolics an additional source of pleasure. In short, all these merely tend to brace them up to an extent the like of which they can scarcely find anywhere else. Thus at this stated season of the year the morning hours are invariably filled with the melodious warblings of certain indigenous birds diversified by the sweet cheering songs of our country maidens and constantly disturbed by the rough crowing of the domestic cock; all of which drag their pleasing length along until the morning dawns upon them and bathes them in the crimson effulgence of the orb of day, driving off the country's face the mist of night which enveloped them in its hazy cover; thus forming the signal for the party to retire to their accustomed abodes for the day's festivities.

The two items described above *viz.*, the swinging process and the beating on the water, have each its own distinctive significance. The former typifies the attempt which these maidens make in order to hang themselves on these instruments and destroy their lives in consequence of the lamented demise of their sexual deity, Kamadevan. It is but natural that depth of sorrow will lead men to extreme courses of action. The beating on the water symbolizes their beating their chests in expression of their deep-felt sorrow caused by their Cupid's death. Such in brief is the description of a Nair festival which plays a conspicuous part in the social history of Malabar. Naturally enough, while within the Christian fold the festive pleasantry and mirth of the Christmas season are going their jolly round, within the limited circle of the Nair society a mournful occasion which time has completely altered into one of mirth, constitutes one of the best enjoyments of our national life.

CHAPTER IX.

FEUDALISM IN MALABAR.

It is an undeniable fact that Malabar has once, in the long period of its chequered history passed through the confusion of Feudalism ; survivals of which remain, though in hazy indistinct forms, down to this day. The *causes* which appear to have contributed to the origin and development of Feudality upon our native soil and the principal *agencies* that have worked to invest it with shape and form were much the same that they were in other quarters of the world that have been caught up by the great feudal wave. *Benefices* and *Commendation* were passed into their service by the people as a protection from the dangerous commotions of the times and this fact goes to sufficiently account for the singular nature of our land tenures and the existence of big landlords in the country. In those troublous times the whole country was distracted by inter-tribal wars and feudal commotions, the stronger preying upon the weaker and in many cases gradually absorbing him. Then people began to place their landed estates in the hands of the more powerful men ; some to receive them back again under subservient tenures, in return for which the former promised to the latter immunity from the imminent dangers of the times ; while others placed themselves and all their property under stronger men's protection and become practically vassals liable to be called out for active service when needed. But it is important to notice that our Feudalism bears closer resemblance to the corresponding continental institution of the thirteenth and the fourteenth centuries than to the same introduced into England by the Conqueror, in that the various petty feudal chieftains were free, independent rulers capable of taking up arms against their feudal head, as we find from Quentin Durward the Duke of Burgundy setting at defiance the feudal authority of his supreme lord, the King of France.

It will be necessary in dealing with the subject to glance, for a moment, at the legendary period of Malabar history so as to clearly trace its gradual yet ceaseless evolution from the times when Parasu Rama miraculously reclaimed it from the sea. This traditional period of Parasu Rama's connection with the country was, in turn, followed for long centuries by a Brahmin theocratical Government. As is wellknown from the recorded traditions of the Puranas, after the reclamation of the country Parasu Rama made a gift of it to the Brahmins in expiation for his sin in exterminating the Kshatriya race, twenty-one times. Hence the land became, even as at this day, a Brahmin country dominated by a Brahmin aristocracy.

Then this Brahmin Theocracy was, for a considerable period, superseded by the reign of the Viceroys of the Pandyan kings as Presidents of Brahmin Republics. Long after, one of these Viceregal Presidents, overcome by lust of independent power, constituted himself independent of his Pandyan surzerain and of his Brahmin councillors and eventually set up a dynasty of his own in Keralam. Then we come to the dawn of authentic history. At this period Malabar was ruled by a line of Princes called Perumals who had their capital at Talicotta near the modern Cranganore. The last of the Perumals became a convert to the Mahommedan faith and embarked for Mecca abdicating his throne and dividing his kingdom amongst his dependents and relatives. This was in A. D. 825. From this year dates the commencement of the present Malayalam era.

At this time the land of Keralam or Malabar was divided into seventeen states ruled by independent princes. The government of these times was mostly on feudal lines. The Rajah of Cochin, the Zamorin of Calicut and other influential royalties of the land were the recognized feudal heads thereof Mr. Wigram says:—"From the earliest times, perhaps before the Aryan migration, there appears to have been a complete military organisation among the Sudras of Malabar. The unit was the *Deshom* presided over by a *Desavali*. A number of Deshoms constitute a *nad* presided over by a *Naduvali* (or Naduvazhi) or local chieftain who was again subject to the Rajah". "The mass of the country called Malabar Proper is divided into a multitude of petty kingdoms or chiefships" says Mr. Grose in his "Voyage to the East Indies." Even at the present day, there are to be met with in the country certain families with traditions such as Ayyayira Prabhu (chief of 5,000 men) and Pathinayira Prabhu (chief of 10,000 men) and many *Naduvazhi* Nayars or rulers of *nad* or country who still possess distinctive rights and privileges over the other members of the Nair sects. They still maintain a fossilized social prominence. They are recognized as belonging to the highest strata of Nair society and are entitled to some social precedence on important festive occasions.. They are mostly jenmies, as may be noticed from the fact that they still retain jenm right over lands though in fearfully encumbered conditions. Some of them are entitled to retinues carrying swords and shields as emblems of a by-gone authority. They are usually addressed not as mere *Nairs*; but by such honorific terms as *Angunnu*. According to Mr. Grœme, a chief was not considered a Naduvali who had not at least a hundred Nairs attached to him. Any number below that ranked a person in the category of a Desavali (or ruler of a Deshom). As there were no taxes in those days each of the chiefs from the Rajah down to the Desavali, possessed demesne lands for their support, which were either cultivated by themselves through their slaves or leased to *Kudians* or tenants. Our modern slave classes found in such comparative abundance in the country are the veritable descendants of the soil serfs through whom cultivation in feudal days was carried on.

Mr. Logan has recorded the following incidents of our old feudal times in his "Manual of Malabar" wherefrom they are taken almost *verbatim* :—

1. The chieftains levied customs duties on *imports exports* and *transports*.

2. He had a recognized *right* to usurp the *estates* of his decaying neighbouring chiefs. "In fact the doctrine of the survival of the fittest was carried into practical politics in Malabar to a great extent."

3. He had the right to force them by violence, if necessary, to contribute supplies on emergencies.

4. Fines of sorts were levied from subjects; and when they died they had their successors particularly those who held offices or rights over land to contribute something in order to ensure recognition of their rights to succeed to the deceased's estate or office.

5. When a man died without heirs the chieftain took his property.

6. No man could adopt an heir without the chief's consent.

7. Presents of congratulation or condolence were always sent to the chieftain on occasions of weddings, funerals, births, openings of new palaces, of ascension to the throne and on the occurrence of numerous other domestic and public events.

8. Leud adulterous women were made over to the chiefs with a premium by the other members of their families in order that they might be taken care of; and the chiefs (or Zamorins at any rate), used in turn to sell

the women to foreign merchants, thus making a double profit out of them.

9. No one might quest for gold without payment of a royalty. Mr. Dillon in his "East Indies" gives a detailed account of this.

10. Under various denomination fees for protection were levied from dependants and strangers; and the levying of such fees from strangers was doubtless one of the obstacles which prevented Fa Hian, the Chinese traveller from penetrating into South India. He wrote :—"Those who desired to proceed thither should first pay a certain sum of money to the king of the country, who will then appoint people to accompany them and shew them the way."

11. Ships which came ashore were annexed by the chieftain of the locality. A still more piratical custom was observed in ancient times. Marco Polo wrote respecting the kingdom of Eli :—"And you must know that if any ship enters their estuary and anchors there having been bound for some other port they seize her and plunder the cargo. For they say you were bound for somewhere else and it is God has sent you hither to us, so we have a right to all your goods; .. and they think it no sin to act thus. And this naughty custom prevails all over those provinces of India, to wit, that if a ship be driven by stress of weather into some other port than that to which it was bound

it is sure to be plundered. But if a ship come bound originally to the place, they receive it with all honor and give it due protection. (Yule's Marco Polo II. 374.) This custom of taking ships and cargoes wrecked on the coast lasted down to recent times; for the English factors at Tellicherry entered into engagements with three of the country powers for exempting English vessels from such seizure.

12. The chieftains held a monopoly of certain animals produced or captured in their domains.

(*a*) *Cows* having an abnornal number of dugs.

(*b*) Cattle that had killed a human being or any animals. They were called red-horns.

(*c*) Cattle born with a white speck near the corner of the eye.

(*d*) Buffaloes with white tips to their nails.

(*e*) Wild elephants caught in pitfalls.

(*g*) The tails and skins of all tigers similarly slain.

(*h*) Wild hogs that had fallen into wells—an occurrence which must have been frequent to judge by the wide area in which this right of the chieftain's was recognized—all these were their perquisites of office.

13. The chieftain's many sources of revenue are given by Mr. Grœme, in his report as special Commissioner for Malabar (1818—1822) One of these may be briefly noticed. In cases of offence given

by one man to another, a duel fight is arranged and fought between the two rival parties; and the chieftain is made the umpire. A sum of one thousand *fanoms* is given as stake or battle wager. These sums went to the chieftain and formed one main source of his revenue. The fighting men may be the champions of each party and not always necessarily the principals in the quarrel.

These all indicate that the great bulk of the people were in those days ruled by chieftains in practically independent bodies, the chieftains, in their turn, owing allegiance to their feudal lords. The Populi were to be at the call of these chieftains who, in turn, were responsible subordinates of the supreme lord. Such was briefly the military organization of the country in ancient days. "The Nairs were in ancient times the militia of the country and held their lands on military tenure liable to be called out at any time for active service. The Rajah of Cochin was the head of this militia in his own country and under him were (Numboorie ?) commandants. When each was able to bear arms he presented the Rajah with a nuzzer and received weapons in return. They were trained to warfare from infancy; but were more inclined to use their arms for purposes of assassination." So says Francis Day.

The absence of taxation lasted down to the times when the Zamorins relinquished their political powers to the British Government which practically rang the death-knell of our feudal sway. Feudal ways and manners survive now only in exceptional forms leaving no distinctive likeness to feudalism as it originally existed here or even in other parts of the world.

With the assumption of authority by the British Government all political power passed to that body leaving its social counterpart in the hands of the old chieftains and lords who retain at the present day only a nominal suzerainty. Thus the old feudal chieftains and lords stripped of their political powers, which at one time they possessed, became, as at the present day, an obsolete and defunct body with no power to enforce their social commandments (which alone they retained in the great transformation of authority) except what they possessed as the lords of the soil or *jenmies*. It is also worthy of note that the chieftains mentioned before had separate estates and rights set apart for them by their feudal lords in return for services they were obliged to render the latter when required; suggestive traces of which are still found in our midst. This reservation of rights and liabilities has also tended to make some of these old chieftains at the present day landlords, big, or small, invested with powers of oppression and domination in the country.

Another feature of the feudal supremacy has reference to authority in matters of marriage. The chieftains possessed also powers over the settlement of marriage within their respective fiefs. The Nairs of any part of the country could not do anything in furtherance of a marriage settlement except under the authority and sanction of the particular chieftain who held sway over that locality. This is still retained though in a visibly weakened form. When a marriage, whether the ordinary Kettu Kallianam or Sambandham or its corresponding institution in parts of the country is arranged to be performed, the first duty of the parties concerned is to pay their respects to their chieftains with proper presents of money and other things, and it is only after the permission of such chieftain is duly obtained that the proposed marriage can be consummated. This old feudal right over the settlement of marriage affairs has also been extended to the performance of other ceremonies and the celebration of festivals. Even in the memory of the present generation there have been instances in which marriages of whatever description have been controlled by such chieftains; and this right has been carried rather too far in some of the interior parts where the chieftain's authority has been perversely exercised in the practising of polyandrism. A wife living with her husband in the genial comforts of married life within such a locality may be the object of attraction and desire by another man who on his petitioning the chieftain with proper presents to allow him to be an extra husband to the said wife gets from the chieftain a duly written social writ which once for all decides the question; in other words the chieftain's authority is exercised in the enforcement of polyandrism. This obtained currency even a generation ago. But now I am not prepared to insist upon the continued existence of the practice.

In certain parts people are not allowed to raise their buildings beyond the first stair lest they should incur the inexorable wrath of their chieftains; departures from this social custom are allowed only with the express consent of the chieftain embodied in a writ of authority issued by him. A like proscription is enjoined in the case of tiling houses. No tiled houses are permitted within the chieftain's feudal area except with his express permission. Such permission is not granted in any and every case. Concessions of this nature are considered indicative of his extreme goodwill.

Likewise certain kinds of conveyances such as *palanquins* and *dholies* are exclusively reserved for the carriage of the feudal heads or chieftains who now survive as nominal royalties. Ordinary men are not permitted to make use of palanquins; but only those social monopolists could take advantage of this privilege, who still possess in other and less honorable ways than in their old days of authority, the means of enforcing this despotic restriction upon low-placed people. But time has wrought in this direction, as in many others, desirable changes; and people have now begun to break through these time-honored traditions by rarely using dholies as conveyances. But I have known no instances in which the *populi* have made use of the palanquin. Certain classes of people were exclusively employed for carrying the palanquins. This class of men goes under the distinctive caste appellation of *Pallichanmar*, (the bearer of *Palli Thandu*, *Palli* being an honorific term and *Thandu*=the handle of these conveyances)—the palanquin or dohli bearers.

Another relic of a feudal custom is also preserved in our marriage institutions. When a tali-tying ceremony is to be performed the girl has to be taken to the chieftain's household with presents of a fixed sum of money and some of the substances prepared for the festival that is to follow. In return the girl is given a golden bracelet which she is then empowered to wear in his or her presence. This latter is symbolical of an authority vested in her ever after to wear this thing in the presence of himself or any one else who is subject to his feudal control. The theory is that no girl who is not thus formally authorized is allowed to wear such ornaments in his presence. In olden times the golden bracelet was given at the cost of the chieftain himself; but later on, a sense of thrift has prevailed and the bracelet has now to be supplied by the girl herself who formally takes it back from the chieftain after it was first put into his hands. The custom bears some analogy to the formal investiture of authority by the Chancellor to graduates presented for the various degrees at University Convocations.

Yet another of these survivals consists in such chieftains conferring certain distinctive caste titles upon his dependents. In Malabar, there exist countless divisions and sub-divisions of castes amongst the people who go by the broad and distinctive name of Nairs. Of these various titles that of *Menon* considered to be of a much higher social order. Hence it is coveted. For a member of some other castes *viz.*, that of *Panikkers* or *Nairs proper* to be promoted to a Menon's estate the process of elevation is exceeding simple and cheap. The man has only to take some presents of money and certain other articles to his chieftain who in the presence of his assembled dependents and others honors the covetous one with the title of Menon. Sometimes a social writ is issued in declaration of this authoritative alteration of a birth-title. Other titles have been, within comparatively recent years, conferred by the chieftains and even by the heads of the old feudal organisations.

In the old feudal days political and social powers were blended and chieftaincy was the symbol of this combined authority. The Chieftains were possessed of even the power of life and death. People paid dearly for their delinquencies. On the slightest provocation and often at the despotic whim of those in authority they were decapitated. In some places all powers both executive and judicial were delegated for a fixed period to natives by the sovereign. This institution was styled *Thalavettiparothiam* or authority obtained by decapitation. *Parothiam* is the name of a supreme authority of those days. The name of the office is still preserved, in the Cochin state, where the village headman is called a *Parathiakaran*. This Thalavettiparothiam was a terrible but interesting institution. It was an office tenable for five years during which its bearer was invested with supreme despotic powers within his jurisdiction. On the expiry of the five years the man's head was cut off and thrown up in the air amongst a large concourse of villagers each of whom vied with the other in trying to catch it in its course down. He who succeeded was nominated to the post for the next five years.

Then, in those days there were what were known as *Mukhiastanmar* who were selected out of the ranks of the villagers and were responsible to the ruling authority for breaches of the law in the village. Night-watchmen were also employed to guard against the entrance into the village of men of suspected character and occupation who could not give satisfactory accounts of themselves. Any one passing by the village in a suspicious manner at night was arrested and locked up by these officials on whom also lay responsibility for the good conduct of the inhabitants of the village. Such officers were appointed for each sub-division of a village, now designated a *Deshom*.

One survival of the feudal times bears upon the early training of young men in the arts of chivalry. Every part of the country contained athletes who could train young men in athletics. The Nairs educated their young men in the arts of war. Special buildings were set apart as training schools where young men from all parts gathered together early in the mornings and were subjected to drill. These youths were first smeared all over with oil and ghee mixed with other substances and were laid prostrate on the ground. Then the training master holding firm in his hand a rope hung downwards from up the roof gently rubbed the student's body with his feet until every available inch of it felt its easy sliding touch. The process continued for one or two hours, and after having been subjected to it for some days the body became quite lissom and almost invertebrate. Every year the student was subjected to this form of treatment. Then he underwent a course discipline and instruction in combats and manœuvring which became complete for all practical purposes after a few years ; and ever after the student armed with a shield and sword was able to meet in single combat a number of people together so trained or untrained. This soldiering institution obtained in all parts of the country and was essential in those days since people had to take special care of life and property. With the lapse of years it has partly decayed and at the present day such an institution in the regular systematic way in which it was in existence before is unknown. But in certain places such training is even now resorted to and availed of during the merry days of Onam or on other equally important national festivals. On the last of the Dusserah days (*Navarathri*) amongst the many other items of education and instruction displayed by the Nairs one consists in the old athletic training described above. Even now there are people who are skilled in gymnastics and wrestling.

There are parts of the country where bracelets can be worn

on both arms only by the Kiriyam and the Sudra castes. Others have to be specially authorized by the local chieftain. Then again it is only these two castes that are allowed to carry about umbrellas with handles, others have to use those made without handles and to wear them on their heads.

In some parts, the lower classes are prohibited from addressing the *communes* as Thampuratti and Thampuran (Queen and King) which, according to the custom, they are obliged to do; these forms of address being the monopoly of the particular chieftain who presides over the social destinies of the locality. The Nairs are generally accustomed to drill a hole in the side of their left nostrils for putting on ornaments therein. Neither of these are they permitted to do in certain places. Even the plantains used for the preparation of curry on festive occasions cannot but cut in a slanting manner, this being exclusively the chieftain's privilege. Of course, travelling beyond the defined bounds of one feudal area into those of another without fear of social ostracism is out of the question. No doubt, these prerogatives may be conceded to the community by the feudal chieftain sometimes as mere acts of grace, at others for prices duly paid.

Some local chieftains hold social sittings for the adjudication of questions that might arise within their respective fiefs; and their decisions are subject to appellate interference by the supreme lords. But in the majority of cases such decisions are made in consultation with the latter. This guarantees their eventual confirmation. Fines are often imposed and collected, the sanction for disobedience being the inevitable wrath of the social authorities and the consequent manifold social troubles which the accused thereafter are made to undergo.

It is interesting to follow a refractory accused when found guilty. On being so pronounced guilty a fine, sometimes amounting to a hundred rupees or more is first imposed on the delinquent. On his refusing or neglecting to pay, he and his whole family are declared social outlaws and are ostracised. Authorised delegates are forthwith despatched in all directions to Enangers and village claimants strictly prohibiting them from attending to the social wants of the proscribed family; it is thereafter left to shift for itself and is practically eliminated from the social economy. But the few families which manage to hold their own against such social autocracy are handled in other and more material ways. Such families together with others which have elected to err with them are promptly evicted of all lands which they may be holding under the offended chieftains and through his influence evicted also of other lands which they may be holding under other chieftains. They are worried in every conceivable way. Thus through the powers which they wield as landlords, the chieftains manage to indulge in an effective exercise of an unquestioned social supremacy inside their feudal jurisdiction; so that one is tempted irresistibly to reflect upon the likelihood of safety remaining for such down-trodden people if the sceptre of political authority were also wielded by such despots. The question will then balance itself between social interdiction and outlawry on the one hand and insecurity of person and property on the other. The cry will then be not as regards equality of rights and representative institutions, but preservation of the most fundamental elements of human existence *viz*, life and property. It is also significant that despite the vigilant supervision of a fostering Government ever anxious about the pettiest details of popular comfort such social despotism is allowed a free sway amidst us even in these days of advancement and liberty; and the sooner measures are adopted for placing an effective check upon such social licentiousness the better for the country.

The chieftains travelled about with attendants both in front and at the back, who carried swords and shields as emblems of power. This practice is followed to this day as the valued relic of an old order of things that has all but wholly vanished. On the advent of the British Government all political power which these petty magnates possessed was absorbed in the social authority which alone could in the stir and confusion of the times firmly maintain its ground. Those old feudal rights are now mostly defunct; and yet the faint echoes of some of them have continued to reach our modern ears. Modern representatives of the old feudal period can only repose in the pleasant belief that their old authority still subsists and that the little power which they still manage to exercise through means, arbitrary and debasing in themselves, is something of which they can legitimately be proud. The facts are that such powers only remain in the reveries of wild imagination. They no longer are concrete entities and no such power can have any valid force or status. The Indian Penal Code contains provisions which if correctly interpreted can be pressed into service by the people against the arbitrary exactions which some chieftains do not scruple to demand and to bridle the capricious exercise of defunct prerogatives. Nevertheless despite all their outworn conditions, some chieftains still manage to exercise portions of such authority through the instrumentality of the powers which they possess as landlords. By means of these powers they still can and do enforce their commands upon the people who, overcome by considerations of the immutable law of self-preservation and expediency, can but succumb to their commands. Lood at in this way the principles of the social reform party are absolutely incapable of maintenance amongst an orthodox set of social despots, with all their honored veneration for the past and with all their deep hatred of innovations however wholesome or necessary. And as such the ultimate destinies of social reform and of the spread of civilisation in our country are surely bound up in those of the Malabar Tenancy Question, a favourable settlement of which alone will bring about social order and social fixity in our old and historic land.

CHAPTER X.

COCK FESTIVAL AT CRANGANORE.

Cranganore is a little sea-port town in the Native State of Cochin. It is bounded on the west by the Arabian Sea, and on the east by a back-water, from which branches a small rivulet which joins the sea running by the south of the town. The western border of this backwater bulges out to a little distance, leaving only a small strip of land to connect the town on the northern side with the mainland; thus, on the whole, giving to the place an almost peninsular character. It is a historic town, with an antiquity stretching back to the beginnings of the Christian era. A Syrian Church is said to have been founded in the mild amusements of this rural retreat during the Eastern Mission of St. Thomas the Apostle. Whatever value may be attached to this account, which is, at best, only traditional, there are associations which have clustered round the town such as would be interesting to the antiquarian. Here are still to be found the remnants of an old dilapidated fortress which admittedly belonged to the days of the Dutch on their first appearance on the west coast of India. Its inhabitants are a peaceful and law-abiding class. Abundance of green fields and luxuriant vegetation lends additional charm to the historic town. The weary traveller finds recreation in the genial puffs of wind which blow gently westward from the backwater, mingling with the bracing breeze which, at sunset, springs up from the sea. The midnight slumber of this lovely place is only disturbed by the solemn moan of the bar, and the rhythmic splash of the boatman's oar as he ploughs his venturous boat through the classic waters of the river. Such are some of the elements of interest attaching to this blessed retreat.

In the midst of its native charms is situated a temple dedicated to Kali, the goddess who presides over the infectious diseases, cholera and small-pox. She is a virgin goddess whom no quantity of blood will satisfy. The temple is an old-fashioned one, presenting no striking architectural peculiarities. The priestly classes attached to it are not, as usual, Brahmins, but a peculiar sect called *Adigals*, of whom there are but three families in the whole of Malabar. The Brahmins are purposely excluded from partici-tion in the poojah ceremonies, lest their extra sanctity might increase the powers of the goddess to a dangerous extent. Poojahs are daily offered to her.

An annual festival known as the Bharani connected with this goddess plays a most important part in the religious history of Malabar. It comes off in the Malayalam month of Meenam (about March or April). Pilgrimages undertaken to the temple on this occasion are potent enough to safeguard the pilgrims and their friends and relations from the perilous attacks of cholera and small-pox. Hence people resort thither annually by the thousands from almost all parts of Malabar; and the more north you go the stronger will you find the hold which the goddess has upon the popular imagination. The chief propitiatory offering on the occasion is the sacrifice of cocks. In fact, every family makes a point of undertaking this sacred mission. People arrange to start on it at an auspicious moment on a fixed day in small isolated bodies. Of course, all the necessaries they take care to carry about their persons. Preparations are made for the journey. Rice, salt, chillies, curry-stuffs, betel-leaves and nuts, a little turmeric powder and pepper, and, above all a number of cocks form an almost complete paraphernalia of the pilgrimage. These are all gathered and preserved in separate bundles, inside a large bag. When the appointed hour comes they throw this bag on their shoulders, conceal their money in their girdles, and with a native-fashioned umbrella in the one hand and a walking-stick in the other they start each from his own house to meet the brother-pilgrims at the rendezvous. Here a foreman is selected practically by common consent.

Then commences the vociferous recitation of that series of obscene songs and ballads which characterises the pilgrimage all along. The foreman it is that opens the ball. He is caught up by others in equally loud and profuse strains. This is continued right up till the beginning of their homeward journey. Nobody whom they come across on the way can successfully escape the coarse Billingsgate of these religious zealots. Even women are not spared.

Perhaps it is in their case that the pilgrims wax all the more eloquently vulgar. A number of cock-feathers are stuck or tied upon the tip of a stick, and with this as a wand they begin to dance and pipe in a set style which is extremely revolting to every sense of decency.

Some of the pilgrims walk out all the distance down to the temple, while others go by boat or some other common conveyances; but in neither case do they deign to spare any passer-by. They usually cook their own meals on the way; which consist of the ordinary rice preparations and plenty of fish and flesh. Hundreds of gallons of

ARRACK AND TODDY

are consumed during the festivals. In short you can hardly find a single sober pilgrim during their continuance. The pilgrims reach the temple in their dirty attire. Their very words smell strongly of a mixture of arrack and undigested animal food. They bathe and have their meals again. The temple premises are crowded to overflowing. The worship of the goddess is then commenced. The offerings consist of the sacrifice of cocks at the temple-altar, turmeric powder, but principally of pepper, as also some other objects of lesser importance. A particular spot inside the temple is set apart for the distribution of what is called manjalprasadam (turmeric powder on which divine blessings have been invoked). The work of doling it out is done by young maidens who are also during the process subjected to ceaseless volleys of vile and vulgar abuse. With surely stoical endurance they submit to attend to their work.

Now, leaving out of account the minor ceremonies, we come to the principal one, *viz*. The sacrifice of cocks.

The popular idea is, the greater the number of cocks sacrificed, the greater is the efficacy of the pilgrimage. Hence men vie with one another in the number of cocks that they carry on the journey. The sacrifice is begun, and then there takes place a regular scramble for the sanctified spot reserved for this butchering ceremony. Now one man holds a cock by the trunk and another pulls out its neck by the head, and in the twinkling of an eye, by the intervention of a sharpened knife, the head is severed from the trunk. The blood then gushes forth in forceful and continuous jets, which is poured directly on a granite piece specially reserved. Then another is similarly slaughtered, and then as many as each of the pilgrims can bring. The same process of butchering is also taken up by thousands of others, and in no length of time the whole of the temple-yard is converted into one horrible expanse of blood, rendering it too slippery to be safely walked over. The piteous cries and death-throes of the poor devoted creatures greatly intensify the horror of the scene. The stench emanating from the blood mixing with the nauseating smell of arrack renders the occasion all the more revolting.

On other higher and more acceptable kind of offering requires more than a passing mention. When a man is taken ill of any infectious disease, his relations generally pray to this goddess for his recovery, solemnly covenanting to perform what goes by the name of

A THULABHARUM CEREMONY.

This is more commonly performed during the Bharani festivals, and I dare say at other seasons of the year likewise. The process consists in placing the patient in one of the scale-pans of a huge balance and weighing him against gold or more generally pepper (and sometimes other substances as well) deposited in the other scale-pan. Then this weight of the substance is offered to the goddess. This is to be performed right in front of the goddess in the temple-yard.

The usual offerings being over, the homeward journey of the pilgrims is begun. But in the meanwhile one remarkable feature remains to be noticed. Though the festival is called Bharani, yet all the pilgrims must vacate the temple on the day previous to the Bharani day; for, from that day onwards the temple-doors are all shut up, and for the next seven days the whole place is given over to the worst depredations of the countless demons over whom this blood-thirsty goddess holds away. No human beings can safely remain there lest they might become prey to these ravenous demons. In short, the Bharani day inaugurates a reign of terror in the locality, lasting for these seven days. Afterwards all the dirt is removed. The temple is cleansed and sanctified, and again left open to public worship.

The pilgrims return, but certainly not in the same manner in which they repaired thither. During the backward journey no obscene songs or expressions are indulged in. They are to come back quietly and calmly without any kind of demonstrations. They get back to their respective homes and distribute the sandals and other pujah substances to their relations and friends who have elected to remain at home ; and the year's pilgrimage is brought to a close.

CHAPTER XI.

THE MALABAR KETTU KALLIANAM.

Our Kettu Kallianam or more properly *Thali Kettu Kallianam* is an important ceremony amongst us. It must be performed before the girl in respect of whom it is celebrated attains puberty. But I dare say there are instances in which it has been put off till after the attainment of age by a girl and in which the girl's Tarawad has in no way suffered. During the progress of the historic legislation concerning Malabar marriages some opponents of the measure based their objections upon the fancied religious nature of Kettu Kallianams and their dignified status as a proper substitute for the kind of marriage which the reformers sought to legalize *viz.*, the legitimate union of the sexes. But this position was found by the eminent members who sat on the said Marriage Bill Commission under the presidency of the late Sir Muthusami Iyer to be so untenable that they felt no compunction in characterizing the ceremony as perfectly useless as a substitute for the other kind of marriage, *viz.*, the lawful wedlock of man and woman. This ceremony has been not inaptly described by some of our native leaders of thought who were examined as witnesses by the said Commission as a "mock-ceremony" possessed of no legal or social force. It is a ceremony at which a string with a small golden *tali* attached to it is tied for the first time round the girl's neck. The several items of it may be briefly detailed as follows: Astrologers are, of course, consulted and an auspicious day and moment are selected for the performance of the ceremony. Then at another auspicious moment a cocoanut tree is cut down for use in connexion with the ceremony, which process is styled "*Puzhuthengu Murikkal.*" This over, a large *Pandal*, a temporary shed, is erected in which to conduct the ceremony and the feasting of guests incident to it. Preparations proportioned to the means of the family are made and guests are invited. Then follows what is popularly called *Ashtamangalliam Vekkal*, that is, the formal opening of the ceremony; which may be done a day before the ceremony or if necessary earlier still. On the day previous to the ceremony the *Attashom* feast is celebrated. On the night of this day, the girl is dressed up in fine clothing and adorned with gaudy ornaments and is led by some of the tribeswomen to a reserved spot inside the house, with flaring torch-lights held in hand by them. Then some ceremonies are performed there attended with singing of songs by the Brahmini woman who is practically the officiating priestess in attendance at the whole ceremony. Then all these together lead the girl to the *pandal* where she is seated with her whole body except the face covered with a piece of fine cloth; and some ceremonies with songs by the said priestess are gone through. The tribeswomen likewise gather round the girl. There may, according to circumstances, be more girls than one for the Kallianam, who may belong to any of the related families of the *clan.* After this comes a sumptuous feasting of guests and others. The place where the girl is seated for the ceremony inside the *pandal* is also a particular one of a square shape with the ground-floor made of clay stirred up and beaten down. Four poles of arecanut timber are stuck on the ground at equal distances and these are also connected on the tops by means of arecanut beams. The roofing of this is made of cotton or silk cloths; and hangings made of tender cocoanut leaves are attached to these beams downwards.

The next day, that is the ceremony-day, the girl is again properly dressed up and adorned and is led a little before the appointed moment to this reserved spot. There she is taken round the square shed three times and is led on to the worship of the sun called *Athithianethozhikkal.* In some places this is done on the bare ground; in others on the top of a terraced shed erected beforehand with four strong pillars and a ceiling of wooden planks. The girl then accompanied by the clanswomen and tribeswomen is taken to the top of this ceiling and is there made to worship the sun. In the meanwhile another process has to be gone through which is designated *mulla kondu varal.* It consists in the carrying in of small stalks of the jessamine plant placed inside a pitcher together with some other ingredients previously taken to a neighbouring temple and consecrated by the performance of a *pooja* by the temple-priest with the pitcher placed near the idol. Inside the pitcher is also placed the tali which is to be tied round the girl's neck. This vessel with the substances in it is brought near the shed, either held in hand by some Brahmin or carried on an elephant's back with drums beating and trumpets blowing. It is then carried up the ceiling and there after some minor ceremonies, consisting of women young and old dancing or playing beneath a bunch made of ears of corn held in their hands over their heads are performed it is taken down the ceiling to the reserved spot inside the *pandal* followed by the girl conducted by the women. In front of the shed and on its western side the girl is seated facing east.

The tier of the tali may be any tribesman or the mother of the girl, any man from amongst the Elayad or Thirumulpad sects or men of the Kiriyam caste. Now the particular person who is to tie the tali, whoever it may be, is then brought down from any neighbouring house where he is seated in readiness for it to the shed inside the *pandal* accompanied by men who indulge in vociferous shoutings all along his way. He is also seated on a chair or a stool behind the girl, dressed in gaudy attire and bathed in shining ornaments of gold. One of the girl's brothers then bathes his feet and afterwards three times the question is put to the village-astrologer who is also in readiness near the *pandal*, whether it is time for the tali to be tied round the girl's neck. Of course, he returns an affirmative answer; and then the person takes the tali and ties it round the girl's neck. Then another tali is similarly tied round the forearm of her right hand by one of her brothers. This practically completes the ceremony. The tying is followed and preceded by sacred ballads sung by the Brahmini woman spoken of before; who mixes the same with the jingling sounds produced by her on a circular thin bell-metal vessel she holds in one hand, by gently striking it with a small metal-rod held in her other. To all these are added, from beginning to end, the rhythmic vociferous shoutings made by parties of men arranged together for the purpose. But one other process yet remains to be noticed. All the while from the moment the girl is led from her seat inside the house up till sho is brought back to her seat there, after all the tedious processes are over, every moment is occupied also with a peculiar sound produced by companies of women by beating their lips rapidly with their fingers of the right-hand and simultaneously forcing their breaths through the lips and the interstices made by the peculiar position of the fingers placed on the lips; so that the whole affair is invested with a kind of dignified solemnity. The tying of the tali practically closes the ceremony and after this a feasting of guests and others takes place.

At this stage it is proposed to give a brief account of a typical Malabar feast, of which the Kettu-Kallianam furnishes a fairly good instance. Preparations are made for it, and invitations are sent out. They are first sent to all clansmen and women, and all *Enangers* (those who belong to the same tribe, but are allowed inter-marriages with the members of the feast-celebrating family) clear eight days before the ceremony; and the smallest delay in sending out the invitation is looked upon as an infraction of the social etiquette, which would sufficiently justify the absence of the guests of the occasion. Under ordinary circumstances, the major portion of the clansmen and tribesmen are bound by social rules to be present on such occasions; failure to do which will be punished by the social chieftains with the imposition of fines. At any rate all the families of the tribe and clan should be represented on the occasions. Strangers are invited only a day or two before the feast. The women all come in one after another dressed in splendid attire and deluged with golden ornaments of divers sorts; and are all seated on mats inside the house or if the house is not sufficiently spacious, inside any temporary shed erected for the purpose. Between about 11 and 12 o'clock in the noon plantain-leaves are spread on the ground, and the guests are all seated on mats to partake of the meal. With regard to the arrangement of the seats certain fixed rules are in vogue. The clanswomen and tribeswomen are first served. Within the sacred precincts of the place where these are seated, no members of stranger clans and tribes and in some cases not even members of higher castes are allowed entrance. Any breach of this social decorum will necessarily result in the guests leaving the hall in a body with their meals left unfinished. Such is the stringency of our caste rules. These are to be served either by Brahmins or other members of their own tribes or clans. These having finished their meals, respectable strangers who have been invited are attended to next. Men comparatively low on the social ladder are seated apart from those on higher ones. This over, the surrounding villagers are served next. But members of stranger villages are often jealously excluded therefrom. Then men of low degree *viz* the mob, including those in every rank of society who have come uninvited are next served. There are no restrictions upon the class of men who are allowed admittance into their ranks. Then come in for their share, the village barber and washerman along with other men of their kind from distances. But they only carry home whatever is given them in the shapes of meal. The other village claimants such as mannans &c., follow them and finally the lowest classes in Malabar society such as the aboriginal tribes are given what little is left after these are all over.

It is a source of extreme satisfaction to find that all animal food and intoxicating drinks are scrupulously excluded from our feasts. But buttermilk is always served at the close of the meals. Our only drink on such occasions consists of pure water boiled with the addition of ginger essentially. Of course, rice properly cooked constitutes the principal element in the whole affair; and the grandness or otherwise of our feasts is determined by reference to the number of *paras* of rice prepared and consumed; all the other ingredients are determined in proportion to the quantity of rice prepared.

Before the determination of a feast an inventory or list is made out theoretically in consultation with the tribesmen; in which the things required are carefully noted down and the subsequent preparations are made on the basis of this inventory. The total cost of a feast is about three times the number of paras of rice consumed. On the evening previous to the feast a preliminary feast called an *Athazom* is celebrated to which only a limited number of guests are invited. But the tribesmen and clansmen are bound to be invited and to be present on that day. The day next after the main feast is called a *vanmuri*, which is also on a small scale; and the kinds of guests to be invited except the tribesmen and clansmen are left to the option of the owner. After a feast is over, what is known as a *pakarcha* is distributed to the families of particular relations and friends; which consists in an impartial distribution to the houses of the latter of some of the most prominent ingredients of the feast. Compared with what obtains amongst the civilized nations our feasts are considerably much cheaper; for what is ours compared with the costly grandeur of an English dinner or a European banquet where gallons of expensive European liquors, and pounds of fish and flesh are consumed; and yet we, as part of the great

Hindu body politic, are often stigmatized as a nation whose chronic poverty is attributed to our lavish waste of money on many an expensive institution, a principal one of which is identified with our national feasts.

In practice the Kettu Kallianam ceremony lasts for the next three days also. But on the second and third days nothing of any importance occurs excepting some dancing and music by young maidens inside the *pandal* and other varieties of amusements.

On the fourth day early in the morning, the members of the various tribes and clans and all specially invited people arrive; and the girl takes an "oil-bath" along with the the women. All of them throughout the occasion are dressed in the most magnificent finery, such as their respective stations in life might permit, and adorned with costly golden ornaments. They all then accompany the girl for worship in a neighbouring temple and after it is over all of them return home. Then they partake of a delicious course of milk conjee with sugar and other ingredients. An hour or two after, another feasting, not in such a splendid style as on the ceremony-day, is celebrated. This over, the ceremony finally closes.

Thus terminates one of the prominent ceremonies connected with our social life. It symbolizes the springing up of a peculiar relationship between the girl and the man who ties the tali; and the man is thereby in some places at least, debarred from marrying her all his life-time, though in other respects he may be eligible. The tali is in some places destroyed on the fourth day. Thus instead of giving the man a right to marry the girl the ceremony destroys even what he previously possessed. Should he die before the girl, which indeed often happens, she must undergo death-pollution and its attendant observances for fifteen days (which the other members of her Tarwad and of her clan either, need not do) just as she should do in the case of the death of one of her own clansmen. It was confusion between this marriage and the legal marriage ceremony recognized amongst all civilized nations that practically formed the basis of the long controversy carried on over the Malabar Marriage Act.

CHAPTER XII.

SERPENT-WORSHIP IN MALABAR.

Malabar is a country which preserves to this day primitive institutions of a type peculiarly fascinating to the ethnologist. Of the various kinds of primitive worship still practised in the country that of the serpent occupies a prominent place. Here the serpent is deified and offerings of poojah are often made to the reptile. It has got a powerful hold upon the popular imagination. Each household has got its own serpent-deity possessing large powers for good as well as for evil. A separate spot is set apart in the house-compound as the abode of these deities. This reserved spot is converted into a small jungle almost circular in shape. It is overgrown with trees of various kinds, and shrubs, and sometimes medicinal plants also. In the middle of this quasi-circular shrine images usually made of laterite after specified shapes are arranged in certain established methods and a passage is opened to the seat of these images from outside. This spot is so scrupulously reserved, that not even domestic animals are allowed to stray therein. No trees from the place are to be felled down, nor any plant whatever for that matter with any metal or more particularly iron weapons; for these are unholy things,

10

the introduction alone of which inside the sanctified area, not to say the actual cutting down of the tree, is regarded as exceedingly distasteful to these serpent-gods. They are not to be desecrated by the touch or even by the approach of a low-caste man. Once in every year at least poojah offerings are made to these gods through the medium of the Numbudri priests.

Periodical ceremonies called *Pambanthullel* are performed to propitiate them. These are resorted to only on special occasions for the purpose of averting serious visitations from the family. The ceremony is a long complicated process. Any individual drawn from among the Nairs themselves are capable of acting the part of priests on these occasions. A day is fixed for the opening of the ceremony; and a particular plot of ground in the house yard is cleansed and preserved for the performance of the poojahs incidental to the ceremony. Then on the spot certain square figures are drawn, one inside another, and these are tastefully diversified by the interpolation of circular figures and others inside and about them, based on geometrical principles. A peculiar symmetry is observed in the matter of these figures. The figures used in the drawings are usually of various colours, red, white, black and others. Ordinary rice-flour, then again such flour mixed with a combination of chunnam and turmeric powder, thereby making the flour pure red, and burnt paddy husk are chiefly employed. Then a number of other accessories are also required for the ceremony in the shape of lamps, cocoanuts, eatables of various sorts prepared from paddy and rice and some other cooked things, such as rice, bread made of rice, and others. These are properly arranged in the place and poojah is offered by the priest with the slow recitation of *mantrams*, and some holy songs or ballads in memory of these gods. Then a number of Nair women, with perfect purity and cleanliness of persons are seated close to each other in a row or two. These women are to preserve sanctity and purity of their persons by a total abstinence from animal food, intoxicants and anything else of an exciting nature for a prescribed period of time; and it is only after the lapse of this period that they become worthy of being admitted to this ceremony. Thus having purged their bodies of all worldliness they are taken into the ceremony and are seated as described before. Now by means of the *mantrams* and poojah the serpent-gods are propitiated and in consequence they manifest themselves in the bodies of these female representatives of theirs. The entrance of the gods into their bodies is characterised by a fearful concussion of their whole frame, gradually developing into a ceaseless shaking, particularly the upper parts. A few minutes afterwards, they begin to speak one by one and their speeches are regarded as expressions of the god's will. Sometimes the gods appear in the bodies of all these females and sometimes only in those of a select few or none at all. The refusal of the gods to enter into such persons is symbolical of some want of cleanliness and purity in them; which contingency is looked upon as a source of anxiety to the individual. It may also suggest the displeasure of these gods towards the family in respect of which the ceremony is performed. In either case, such refusal on the part of the gods is an index of their ill-will or dissatisfaction. In cases where the gods refuse to appear in any one of these seated for the purpose, the ceremony is prolonged until the gods are so properly propitiated as to constrain them to manifest themselves. Then after the lapse of the number of days fixed for the ceremony and after the will of the serpent-gods is duly expressed the ceremonies close.

One other small item of offering to these gods consists in certain ballads sung by the Pulluvar females going about from house to house at stated seasons of the year. They take a pretty large pitcher, close its opening by means of a small circular piece of thin leather which is fastened on to the vessel by means of strings strongly tied round its neck. Another string is adjusted to the leather-cover which when played on by means of the fingers, produces a hoarse note which is said to please the god's ears, pacify their anger and lull them into sleep. This vessel is carried from house to house in the day time by these Pulluvar females; and placing the vessel in a particular position on the ground, and sitting in a particular fashion in relation to the vessel, they play on the string which then produces a very pleasing musical note. Then they sing ballads to the accompaniment of these notes. After continuing this for sometime they stop, and getting their customory dues from the family, go their own way. It is believed that these notes and the ballads are peculiarly pleasing to the serpent-gods, who bless those for whose sakes the music has been rendered. In consequence of the halo of sanctity that has been popularly thrown round the serpent it is considered a sin of a most heinous nature to kill one of these deified reptiles. The killing of a cobra is ragarded with the utmost concern amongst us. In such case the carcase is taken and duly burned with all the necessary solemn ceremonials. Sandal-wood is the fuel used sometimes. A small pit is dug which is covered with sandalwood pieces and they are set fire to. When the flame burns intensely the body is quietly placed in it, and reduced to ashes together with, in some cases, incense and myrrh. This is believed to mitigate the dangers consequent on the death of the serpent.

The popular conception of the family-cobra is that it is a tiny little thing with a full devēloped hood, and fangs, and possessing a golden tinge; which shine brilliantly in the rays of the sun. At the sight of human beings it gets away to its holy shrine exhibiting a reeling motion on its way thither. It never gets far away from its abode of which it is the perennial guardian.

One striking phase of serpent-worship in Malabar relates to the family of *Pappanmakkat Nambudris* and the singular and effective control they exercise over serpents in general. Their powers are handed from father to son. It is said that this Nambudri household is full of cobras which find their abode in every nook and corner of it. The inmates can scarcely move about without placing their feet upon any one of these serpents. Owing to the magic influence of the family the serpents cannot and will not injure them. The serpents are said to be always at the beck and call of the members of this Numbudri family and render unquestioned obedience to their commands. They watch and protect the interests of the family in the most jealous spirit. In short, these reptiles live, move, and have their being as freely as if they were domesticated animals imbued with supernatural powers.

Cases of cobra-poision are generally taken to this Brahmin family and the headman sometimes summons before him the identical animal which caused injury and it is said successfully effects a cure as if by some mystic and magic influence.

The serpent also plays a conspicuous part in contracts between citizens. The family-serpent is in old deeds the subject-matter of sale. The sale of a house compound extends also to the family-serpent. The stipulation in these documents invariably is that the family-serpents are sold along with the properties; and even in cases of division of family property amongst its several branches of members, the family-serpent is included in the division. Such is the sacred prominence which has been given to the serpent amongst us. Their anger is said to manifest itself in some member of the family being struck down with leprosy or some other loathsome disease; while by their propitiation they can be converted into the guardian angels of our households, powerful enough to preserve the prosperity of the imates as well as to vouchsafe their complete immunity from the attacks of virulent diseases and sometimes even from death.

CHAPTER XIII.

SOME DEPRESSED CLASSES OF MALABAR.

The question of the depressed races of the inhabitants of Malabar is a very interesting and important one, and deserves the serious attention of all who are interested in its social history. These people constitute our unquestioned aborigines, a study of whose racial life, manners and institutions, and a permanent record of them, will form a useful addition to the ethnological literature of the world. They are every year increasing in numbers, and threaten to swamp the country. The miseries incidental to their depraved conditions of existence are untold; and the problem of the amelioration of that condition is every moment gathering additional prominence, much like the Pariah problem of the East Coast. They may be variously designated as *Cherumas*, *Pulayas*, *Kanakkars*, *Pariahs*, *Malayar* and *Kadar*, *Naidis*. There are also one or two more of these races found in parts of the country; but they present much the same tribal peculiarities as those I have enumerated. I will now proceed to dispose of these in the order which their social circumstances seem to justify.

The *Cherumas* are a numerous race, and are styled in the vernacular *Cherumukkal;* their name importing that they are sons of the field (from *Chera*,—dam. and *Mukkal*—children). They are born and live mostly on the fields. They are a very inferior race and are regarded merely as agricultural instruments in the hands of the landlords, their masters, who supply them with houses on their estates and work them in a way little better than that in which they utilize their live stock. Their daily maintenance is supplied to them by their masters themselves. Every morning the master's agent summons them to his house and takes them away to work in the fields, in ploughing, drawing water from wells, and in short doing the whole work of cultivation. In the evenings a certain quantity of paddy is distributed to them as wages. Both theory and practice, in the great majority of cases, are that they are to be fed at the master's cost the whole year round, whether they work in the fields, or not. But it is very seldom that they can have a holiday, regard being had to the nature of agriculture in Malabar. Their children are trained from an early age in the work of their elders.

Their houses are little huts, generally built of bamboo and thatched with straw, or a particular variety of dried grass found in great abundance on the hill-sides. Earthen pots constitute their only domestic utensils. Some of them live far from the fields; while others live, particularly during the rainy season, on the fields themselves, in small huts on the field-sides, or on the big earth mounds which separate them.

They are divided into families and practically have no recognised racial chiefs to safeguard their interests and to hold them together. But there are certain assemblies of elders, with a kind of chief at their head, invested with certain powers for the adjudication and settlement of disputes.

Their staple food is the rice which they obtain as wages; but any deficiency in the food which their daily wages bring them they make up in other ways, as by eating roots, fish, etc. Toddy forms their main article of drink. They do not eat carrion; but are extremely fond of fish, which, cooked in the poorest fashion, they reckon a delicacy. They have no peculiar customs worth recording. Their whole life is spent in cultivation, and they show no taste for hunting or other pastimes. They are a debased and ignorant race, as timid as hares at the approach of human beings. On all important festivals of the year they collect at the master's house and are given each a fixed quantity of rice or paddy, with other articles and a small coarse piece of cloth to serve as a dress for the whole of the ensuing year. Their personal appearance is forbidding. They are a dark, muscular race, with much of their natural muscularity adversely affected by their scanty food and poor clothing. Their one piece of cloth they tie round their waists. They wash this only once or twice in the year; but, their work being mostly in the fields and in the open it gets washed, with their bodies, in the constant rains which fall during the monsoon. During the height of the season they protect themselves from its biting cold by means of the fires which they burn inside their huts all night long and often throughout the whole day.

Their chief ornaments are, for males, large bunches of earrings and sometimes rings on the fingers. But the women are adorned with nose and breast ornaments, and rings on the fingers and even on the toes. It is worthy of note that all these ornaments are invariably made of brass. The razors with which they shave are in some instances rude iron knives which, during the operation, subject them to intense pain. Some of these races wear a front tuft, while others shave the head clean. Their females do all the cooking and take care of the children; but often they accompany their males to the fields and do such work therein as they are capable of.

They are a dolico-cephalic race, with medium-sized eyes and dark complexion. They follow the *makkathayam* line of inheritance, or descent through the fathers; and their household consists mostly of husband and wife and their children, if any. Polygamy, polyandry and divorce are unknown amongst them.

They worship certain gods, who are represented by rude stone images. What few ceremonies are in force amongst them are performed by priests selected from their own ranks, and these priests are held in great veneration by them. They kill cocks as offerings to these deities, who are propitiated by the pouring on some stones placed near them, of the fresh blood that gushes forth from the necks of the birds. Their dead are disposed of by burying. The whole race without exception are believers in the existence of a God, who, to their rude imagination, lives in the stone images of their deities ; and some of them believe also in a life beyond the grave, while others believe in the total extinction of the individual, his spirit being annihilated along with the body.

The *Pulayas* are a variety of *Cherumas*, as also are the *Kanakkars* ; but the latter can approach a high-caste man more closely than the other two without pollutiug him. These latter share the racial characteristics of the *Cherumas* and *Pulayas* and are a purely agricultural class living and working in the fields. The *Kanakkars* shave their heads clean like Native Christians, whereas the other two retain the frontal tufts like the Nairs. All three are an extremely loyal class of people, devotedly attached to their masters, whose interests they watch and protect most jealously., On the death of any member of the master's household their families collect in the vicinity of his house and mourn the loss by beating their chests and crying aloud till their sorrow is assuaged, quite as naturally and unaffectedly as if the loss were personal to them.

The existence of these three races furnishes an instance of practical slavery in our midst, even in these days of advancing civilization. They are believed to be the slaves of their masters, who frequently subject them to inhuman punishments in case of disobedience or negligence; and their master's commands and deeds are invested with a certain sanctity and inviolability in their eyes. They are the master's property, and can be sold away or otherwise dealt with at his will. The fact is that these slaves, or their ancestors more correctly, were purchased in days of yore by the masters or their ancestors for a fixed price, and hence originates the latter's unchallengable authority over them. Any slave running away from his legitimate owner and joining the working ranks of another master, if caught, is subjected to brutal punishments at the hands of the former master. In the view of some people, such improper admission of a renegade slave is against the law. But such views are only theoretical in our days, and are no longer within the realm of reality.

The slavish nature of these races is illustrated by the following and like forms of address employed by them. They still speak of themselves in the presence of superior races as *Adiyangal*, *i.e.*, he who lies at (your) feet. When speaking of their eyes, hands or other members of their bodies, they are required to call them *old eyes*, *old hands*, &c. So also with *rice*, which they mention as *stone*-rice. Their children are all *kidangal*, or calves, and their silver money is *copper* cash, or *chempin kasu*. They call all Nairs *Thanpurans*, or kings. These and many other curious forms of address used by them irresistibly point to the prevalence of an idea amongst them that they are only slaves, and their masters lords capable of doing anything with them. It is enough to say that, though their emancipation was effected as far back as A.D. 1854 yet it has only been nominal, and has not yet been carried out in its entirety; and people even now speak of slaves in some places, quite forgetting that the political doctrine of human equality and fraternity has been authoritatively insisted on since the advent of the British Government.

The Parayas come next among the races of extremely depressed life and habits. They are a lower caste of slaves and more degraded, and their occupation is less honourable than that of the other slaves. They keep their top-knots, like the Nairs, and shave the rest of their heads. They are also a dolico-cephalic race with sturdy muscular frames, dark complexion, comparatively thick lips, and a detestable odour. In some places they are utilized in agriculture, but more generally their occupation is of other kinds. They live mostly neither in the fields, nor on the mountains, but in the plains and only in some rare instances on the mountains. They live in small houses built of bamboo and thatched with cocoanut or palmyra leaves, or with straw of dried grass; but in any case their habitations do not afford sufficient accommodation for more than two or three souls, or at most one family. They are notorious toddy-drinkers and do not eat carrion; but those who live on cocoanut plantations eat beef boiled without salt and chillies. Their chief food is rice, which they obtain during the day. Their meals are cooked in earthen pots of very rough patterns. They are very fond of ornaments. Earrings for their ears, rings for their fingers, are the chief of those worn by males; but the females have the whole body loaded with brass ornaments. According to a popular tradition, the Parayas are a race of Brahmin extraction, being descended from a Brahmin woman. They are to this day said to possess Brahmin characters and traditions, and some of them are professed *mantravadis*, or magicians, and are credited with tremendous powers over certain evil spirits or demons and sought after in their mountain abodes by those who desire to wreak vengeance upon their enemies. There are minor *mantravadis* amongst those who live on the plains, too, whose services are availed of in casting out less powerful devils from the bodies of persons possessed. In the case of the more powerful of such magicians the process of obtaining their services is very simple. People visit these magician *Parayas* in their dwellings and they enter into mutual compacts, the former covenanting to pay a fixed sum of money and the latter pledging themselves to bring about the death of the enemy. Thenceforth all sorts of evil incantations are performed by the magician to accomplish the agreed result. Another and more inhuman way in which sorcery and witchcraft are resorted to by these magicians has a very curious ring about it. His aid being sought after against an individual, the magician goes through all the required preliminaries and on the last day, accompanied by one or two assistants, he goes at night, in the disguise of a dog, or a cow. or ox, or other animal near the house where the victim is sleeping. The latter forthwith opens the door and walks out of the house. When he comes out, he is caught and is murdered, by breaking his neck, or in some other brutal fashion. This cruel practice is generally attributed to the Paraya caste of people. But it is practised by others as well.

In certain places there are temples dedicated to the subordinate deities of the goddess Kali. At certain appointed periods of the year these Parayas have to assume the garb of an evil deity, with large head-dresses and paintings on the body and face and tender cocoanut-leaves hanging loose around their waists, all these embellishments being of the rudest patterns. With figures such as these, terror-striking in themselves, dancing with tom-toms sounding and horns blowing, representing the various temple deities, they visit the Nair houses, professing thereby to drive off any evil deities that may be haunting their neighbourhood. After their dues have been given them they go their ways; and, on the last day, after finishing their house-to-house visits, they collect near their special temples to take part in the *Véla* tamash.

Some of the *Parayas* employ themselves in making umbrellas with palmyra leaves for coverings and small bamboo-sticks for handles; and also in making large and tough mats of long thin pieces of bamboo material.

The *Parayas* are mostly believers in evil deities, whom they worship and control for personal services; and they are also believers in the existence of a personal God, who presides over their destinies. Their deities are represented by rude stone images which they place in their temples. Their chief article of clothing is a small cotton cloth tied round the waist. Bathing is an institution almost unknown amongst them. They shave with rough metal blades. The *Paraya* is allowed to approach a high caste Hindu only at a distance somewhat greater than that allowed in the case of the three races of our slave population mentioned above.

The *Vettuvar* are a sect of people who are not exactly slaves, but whose social position justifies their classification amongst the slave races. They are confined to particular parts of the country, and live on the cocoanut plantations of the Nairs and other well-to-do-classes. They are not, like the other races described above, an agricultural people; but are only workmen, leading a hand-to-mouth existence on the wages which they obtain for hedging and fencing cocoanut plantations, plucking cocoanuts therefrom, tilling them, and doing other allied kinds of work.

They live with their wives and children, and sometimes other relations as well, in houses small but more decent-looking than the mere huts of the other slave classes. In point of caste restrictions they are certainly better circumstanced; and their daily contact with the higher classes in the ordinary concerns of life affords them greater facilities for increased knowledge and civilization than their brother-citizens of the slave races enjoy.

They are much addicted to toddy-drinking; but their principal food is rice. Their condition is never so intolerably wretched as that of the other classes. They are sometimes employed by cultivators for agricultural purposes. Their females occupy themselves in the fields during the harvest season, but they do other kinds of work as well, such as making thatchings for houses with cocoanut leaves woven after a set model during the thatching season about December or January.

Their males wear earrings of brass and their females adorn themselves with nose, finger and chest ornaments of brass or beads. The one piece of cloth supplied to them annually by the masters to whose plantations they are attached, forms their dress, both for males and females, which they tie round their waists. They do not eat carrion, but are exceedingly fond of fish, the flesh of the civet and the rat, and of some other animals not generally eaten by other classes of people. They observe death-pollution just as the higher classes of Malabar, and the period of observance varies according to the particular class or caste to which their masters belong. For instance, if they belong to a Nair's plantations, such period in 15 days; and if to a Brahmin's it is 10 days, Nairs and Brahmins observing pollution for these periods respectively. The priests who officiate at their ceremonies are selected from among their own tribesmen called *Enangers*; whose express recognition is necessary to give validity to the performance of the ceremony.

Their marriage customs present no striking peculiarities, and are very much like those of the *Tiyyars*, excepting that the feasting and revelry are not so pompous in their case, they being a much poorer race than the *Tiyyars.*

Like the Nairs, they retain the front knot. But they are an extremely unclean race. The only offences of general occurrence amongst them are petty cases of theft of cocoanut, plantains, areca nuts and roots of common consumption amongst us. But in the case of the other races theft is not of such common occurrence.

The *Vettuvars* also believe in a Supreme Creator, whom they name and invoke as *Paduchathampuram*, *i.e.*; the King who created (us), even in their ordinary utterances. Likewise they believe in certain evil deities to whom they make offerings at particular times of the year. They are not like the other classes, distinguished by loyalty or attachment towards their masters ; but are a very ungrateful sect, and their very name, *viz.*, a *Nambuvettuvan*, or a *Vettuvan*, or a *Namban*, has passed into a bye-word for " ingratitude" of all kinds.

Next there are the purely hill-tribes whose abodes are confined to the tops of mountains and hills. They are mainly the *Malayars* and the *Kaders*, and also the *Naidis.*

The *Malayars* (from Mala = mountain) means the men of the mountains. " The *Malayars* and the *Kaders* are identical races living about the western and eastern sides of the ghauts respectively. In point of national characteristics, they partake of the nature of the aborigines of the country, and the Hindus of the plains above which they are found in a topographically ascending and a socially descending scale."

The *Malayar* language is a felicitous combination of Tamil and Malayalam, diversified here and there by the admixture of certain singular provincialisms. Their pronunciation is of a curious kind. The *Malayars* are socially superior to the *Kaders*, who are little better than savages. In physical appearance even the slaves are inferior to the *Malayars*. Each community of the Malaya sect has its own chief, who collects the dues from them and arranges their barter for them.

They mainly subsist on rice, wild game and arrowroot, and occupy themselves in the cultivation of small spots of *rali*, and in felling timber and firewood, which fetches them something to live upon.

Their main occupation is collecting honey and beeswax, and they are also famous as trackers in jungles, by which pursuits they manage to make up any deficiency in their means of subsistence. Like some of the slave classes they are exceedingly fond of toddy, which they consume in large quantities.

Their ornaments consist of a long string of beads tied round the neck. Their women also are fond of ornaments; and usually wear strings of white and red beads round their necks, bangles on their arms, and rings on their fingers and often on their toes. Rigid endogamy is enforced amongst them, they marrying within their own village. Polygamy is absolutely unknown amongst them; but divorce is freely allowed for infidelity on the part of the wife; though it is a matter for eventual settlement by the villagers. When a wife is so divorced by the husband, she is not afterwards taken back by him; but may be re-married to another man. But cases of divorce are extremely rare. Their marriage customs have something peculiar about them. At a marriage, feasting of guests takes place at the expense of the bridegroom's father; and after the conclusion of the marriage he makes a small gift to the girl's mother and only a present to the daughter for her to buy a new dress with. The pair then proceed to a newly-built cottage erected as their future place of residence, where they spend the rest of their lives in such little comfort as they can derive from their straitened circumstances.

They believe in a Supreme Diety who presides over their destinies and supplicate Him through their tribal god who is called a *Mullung*, which is a stone placed inside a circular wall erected for the purpose. It may be surmised that they are practically an ancestor-worshipping class, the spirits of their various ancestors being represented by a collection of stones, one for each. Such spirits are invoked for help and protection from calamities of all kinds. Towards the month of April they offer sacrifices of honey and sometimes of goats; and failure to do this is believed to bring about their destruction by tigers and wild elephants.

One peculiar custom amongst them requires special notice. They repose a profound belief in the evil powers which they are capable of exercising over one another through their evil deities, who are their guardian angels. Hence, when one of them finds wax or honey on a particular tree, he takes special care to examine its bark, to see whether it bears any sign made by another in indication of its previous discovery and appropriation by him, in which case he religiously abstains from taking out the honey or the wax, lest any evil influence should be exercised on him by the previous finder. This scrupulous observance of the sanctity of possession by them seems to account for the comparative scarcity of crime in *Malayar* life.

The diseases they commonly contract are not numerous. It is not strange that, living, as they do amidst mountainous surroundings, and breathing the poisoned air of those regions they are subject to attacks of malarious fever; but they are their own physicians, who can cure themselves, and cases of fever are not very frequent; nevertheless, they are subject to constant attacks of cholera. They are also believed to be powerful snake-charmers and to be able to effect cures in cases of cobra poisoning, with a green leaf administered internally to the patient, and applied externally to the part affected by the bite. They bury their dead, instead of cremating them.

The Malayar houses are of a peculiar pattern. They are

raised on clumps of bamboos, which are all cut about the middle to the same height so as to produce an even surface high up from the ground. This surface is then converted into a sort of flooring by spreading planks closely all over it, and over the planks a thick layer of mud is beaten down and rendered firm. Then other planks are fixed perpendicularly to the four sides of the flooring, in a closely set order, so as to serve as walls. Over these latter is again put a roofing of planks, and openings are made in the walls, thus making a stronghold against the devastations of wild animals. Entrance to this dwelling is facilitated by means of a ladder made by cutting away the knots from a single bamboo outside the clump, and leaving only the root ends of these knots to serve as stairs or steps to descend or ascend by. The *Malayars* keep in their custody all the year round a number of very strong bows and a cluster of arrows with slightly spread out and sharpened iron ends; some of which are kept always ready in their furnaces to be shot red hot at wild animals that approach them. They kill the game, bring it home, flay it, and dry it in the sun so as to preserve it for winter living. The *Malayars* are extremely devoted towards their masters, the owners of the mountains where they take up their abodes. They make presents to them occasionally of honey and wax. Instances are common in which they have shot and killed lonely passers-by in the neighbourhood of their mountain abodes and robbed them of all their belongings. They are a sturdy, muscular race, endowed with tremendous physiques; and their bows, their ordinary weapons of offence and defence, are incapable of being bent to any appreciable extent by our strongest-built men.

The *Kaders* are a socially inferior race to the *Malayars* and are found in the higher ranges of the ghauts; their most famous divisions occupying the summits of the Anamalai and Kollengode ranges. They are a short, muscular race of deep black colour, with thick lips like Negroes, but without the detestable smell of the latter. The *Kader* language is Tamil; and their various dialects are so curious and difficult that even Tamil-speaking people cannot correctly understand them. They are all under the control of a headman who is also an authoritative referee in all their disputes. He also performs all their priestly functions, and receives in return a fixed portion of the proceeds from certain large trees and a certain percentage of the honey and wax collected by them. Their women wear dark-coloured clothes, or clothes rendered dark by their unclean life and habits; as well as beads, charms, rings and bangles. They are a lazy race, much averse to manual labour; but they are excellent at tracking game in jungles and in collecting wild produce therefrom; and they are also experts in finding good timber for purpose of felling. Their houses are collections of small hovels made of branches of trees covered over with leaves. They live upon trapped animals, wild yams, bamboo seed and other wild productions of the jungles. They also eat rice, which they obtain as remuneration for collecting wax and honey. They first remove all poisonous particles from wild yams by cutting them into small pieces and leaving them to soak in a running stream of water. During the winter season they consume arrowroot in abundance. They mix honey with arrowroot meal, place the mixture in the hollow of a piece of wild bamboo and sink the same inside the floor of their houses where it gets hard, forming a kind of sweetmeat.

Their methods of collecting honey and wax are worthy of detail. They carry on this business only at night time. One of them goes out with a basket hanging loose from his neck by means of a string and a glaring torch held in his hand, and ascends the tree on which the hive has been discovered, on pegs driven in one above another up to the point where the hive has been found. On seeing the torch, the bees get frightened and fly away, leaving the hive behind. Then the hive is taken out and is brought away in the basket carried on the neck. But if the honey or wax be found on a rock or a precipice, the process is different. A ladder is made of long canes stripped of the outer covering and twisted together. This is then hung down the rock or precipice, and by means of it the men climb down. It is in ways such as these that both the *Malayars* and *Kaders* collect honey and wax.

Strict monogamy is enforced among them. No relation on the male side is allowed to be taken to wife. Their marriage customs are somewhat peculiar. The man who intends to marry goes out of his own village and lives in another for a whole year, during which period he makes his choice of a wife. At the end of the year he returns to his own village and obtains permission from the villagers to effectuate the contemplated union. Then he goes away again to the village of his bride-elect and gives her a dowry by working there for another whole year. Then he makes presents of clothes and iron tools to the girl's mother; after which follows a feast which completes the ceremony. Finally the couple return to the husband's village. Amongst the *Kader's* re-marriage of widows is freely allowed. In this important respect they may be said to be ahead of the conservative Hindus, whose orthodoxy is an insuperable barrier in the way of their national advancement. For conjugal infidelity the wife has to pay a fine to the husband. This practically converts adultery on the part of the wife into a source of income to the husband. If, in any case, the girl happens to make a fugitive connexion with any man, then the tribesmen assemble together, and, on the case being proved to their satisfaction, they unanimously compel the guilty man to take the girl as his wife.

Their temples consist of small huts inside which are placed rude stones which represent their deities who protect them from the depredations of wild animals, as also from misfortunes of any kind befalling them. During the Vishu festival they come down and visit the plains with the *Malayars*, and on their way they worship and pray to any image they chance to come across. They are believers in the supernatural efficacy of witchcraft and attribute all diseases to the miraculous workings of that art. The *Kaders* are good exorcists themselves and trade in *Mantravadams*, or magic. Like the *Malayars*, they bury their dead.

Being acclimatized to the jungle-poisoned atmosphere of their native abodes, they enjoy practical immunity from attacks of fever, but when they change their dwellings to the plains they become subject to such diseases.

The lowest race of people in Malabar are known by the name of *Naidis*, *i.e.*, hunters (from *Nayaduka*=to hunt). They are a wandering class of people of disgustingly unclean habits, and so impure in their persons, food and dress, that hardly any member of the multifarious castes of Malabar will condescend to touch them. They are strictly prohibited from appearing within some hundreds of yards of a high caste Hindu. They drag out an extremely miserable existence in wretched hovels and subsist upon what they can get for watching crops against wild animals, and in the shape of charity from people passing by, to whom they ceaselessly yell and howl out till they obtain something from them. They entertain an intense dislike for manual labour; but are sometimes employed by sportsmen to serve as beaters. They subsist mainly upon roots and possess no knowledge of trapping animals or snaring birds. They also eat oysters, tortoises and crocodiles, which latter they capture by means of ropes and hooks. The flesh of these animals they bake and eat without the addition of salt and chillies. They seldom wash being prohibited from touching water (or even climbing trees) for which offences they have to fast for a whole day. They generally cover their nakedness by tying round their waists long strings made of leaves and plants; but some make use of clothes for the purpose. They are naturally possessed of loud voices, and, as already stated, yell out for charity. Many of them become converts to Christianity, or more frequently Mahommedanism, which practically shortens their distance of approach to the high caste population.

These *Naidis* employ themselves in the construction of ropes and slings with coir, yarn, etc. They live around the base of the ghauts and on the sides of the hills scattered over the various parts of the country. Some of them occupy themselves in collecting beeswax, gums, etc., from trees and bushes. Their marriage customs are simple and interesting. A large hut is constructed of holly and other leaves, inside which the girl is ensconced. Then all the young men and women of the village gather round the hut and form a ring about it. The girl's father, or the nearest male relative, sits at a short distance from the crowd with a tom-tom in his hands. Then commences the music, and a chant is sung by the father which has been freely translated as follws :—

" Take the stick my sweetest daughter,
Now seize the stick my dearest love,
Should you not capture the husband you wish for,
Remember 'tis fate decides whom you shall have."

All the young men who are eligible for the marriage arm themselves with a stick each and begin to dance round the little hut inside which the bride is seated. This goes on for close on an hour, when each of them thrusts his stick inside the hut through the leaf-coverings. The girl has then to take hold of one of these sticks from the inside, and the owner of whichever stick the girl seizes becomes the husband of the concealed bride. This ceremony is followed up by feasting, after which the marriage is consummated. A girl once married can never after be divorced.

They worship a female deity, and about the month of March sacrifice a cock as a means of protecting themselves from all evils. They are credited with prophetic powers. When a man lies at the point of death, it is usual to distribute rice *kanji* to these people, who, after eating their fill, become seized with the power of predicting the fate in store for the sick man. According as the taste of the *kanji* turns to that of a corpse, or remains unaltered, the death or recovery of the patient is foretold in their deep and loud voices.

It is worthy of note that the line of descent recognized amongst these classes is *Makkathayam* *i.e.*, through sons or males. This fact *apparently* rebuts the presumption that the Malabar *Marumakkathayam*, or succession through females, finds its origin in the universal law of female descent which, as a necessary first step in the world's social history, is still found prevalent amongst various primitive races. The origin of female descent in Malabar is exclusively attributable to

Nambudri Brahmins, who, from considerations of policy and necessity, have instituted this peculiar custom of reckoning descent through the female side. It is argued in this connexion, that, if the origin of our female descent is to be sought in the universal law, then in the natural course of things such a custom should have survived amongst these depressed orders, who, as the recognized aborigines of Malabar would have preserved their primitive method of descent, *i.e.*, through females. But since they follow the male line in matters of succession, the origin grounded on universal law has no valid foundation. As I have already on a former occasion discussed this question, I do not recapitulate my reasons in support of my position. But I refer to it here only with a view to showing that there are points of antiquarian or ethnological interest connected with these primitive types of human kind.

As has already been pointed out, all the races numbered amongst the depressed classes are known to reckon their descent through the male side. There is some difficulty in ascertaining this, by reason of their extreme poverty, which renders them devoid of any property in regard to which any succession may be recognized. But this difficulty may be got over by seeing which of the parents becomes the possessor of their children, who maintains them and the mother, and where the mother remains after marriage. In this connection, it may be noted that it is the father who maintains the mother and children; it is in the husband's house that the wife lives after marriage, and it is the father that retains possession of the wife and children throughout their lives, and the children's relations on the maternal side have nothing to do with them beyond visiting them occasionally during the year. Hence the presumption is that it is the male line of descent that these people follow.

In connection with our subject it is impossible not to speak of the indefatigable efforts which the mission agencies are putting forth towards the social up-lifting of these races. The motives of these benefactors of mankind are truly laudable. By considerable self-sacrifice, and energy, they are preaching the Christian gospel in remote areas and are receiving many, within the fostering embrace of Christianity. Thus they attempt by every means in their power to raise the social condition of these races and render them capable of approaching more closely to high caste Hindus. The conventional caste restrictions are hopeless impediments in the way of their personally representing their extreme wretchedness to the moneyed Hindus, from whom alone they can expect to derive any sensible relief. Acceptance of Christianity, besides conferring other boons upon these races, also considerably enhances their freedom of movement from place to place which otherwise is beset with great obstacles. They have to make a long circuit to avoid the high caste passer-by if they happen to meet each other from the opposite ends of a fenced path way. Such and similar are the inconveniences and difficulties incidental to their depraved condition. The bare removal of these disadvantages must, in itself, be a source of a great relief to these miserable specimens of humanity. The wretchedness of their condition is accentuated by the fact that wages are miserably low in Malabar, being about two annas and even less. There are, again, masters in the country who treat them little better than the old Romans did their slaves, allowing them only a pittance in the shape of wages and at the same time maltreating them by the cruel administration of severe caning and other forms of oppression, after trying them up to trees. These cruelties are practised only in the interior of the land, not visibly affected by the healthy influences of British officialism. The rapid and dangerous strides with which these races are increasing in numbers, coupled with the poor and meagre wages that their masters dole out to them and their cruel maltreatment are matters which claim the earnest attention of every true lover of peace and reform.

CHAPTER XIV.

VILLAGE LIFE.

The village life of Malabar is delightfully charming and simple. It is rapidly passing off under the influences of western civilization; and as such it is only right and proper to attempt to preserve a lasting account of it at this important epoch of transition.

I begin with our *village education.* There are two kinds of village teachers *viz.*, those that are maintained by leading families on small monthly allowances and meals; and those who maintain village schools on their own account and live upon the income derived therefrom. These teachers are usually called *Ezhuttachans* and the schools themselves, *Ezhuttupallis.* The education of our youths commences at a very early period of their lives. On some auspicious day and at some auspicious moment the commencement is made. Oftentimes this is done on the *Vidyarambham* day in the month of Kanni or Tulam. A fairly well-educated man is first selected to give the boy his first lesson. A quantity of raw rice is kept in a bell-metal vessel, and a lamp is kept burning in front of it. Two measures consisting of rice and paddy respectively are also placed each on either side of this vessel. The boy scarcely four or five years old is seated in front of the vessel, and the *Guru* spoken of before takes a gold *Fanom* (an old coin) and writes on the boy's tongue the divine invocation *viz.*, Hari - Sri - Ga - Na - Pa - Ta - Ye-Na - Ma. He then catches hold of the boy's index finger and makes him to write the same thing on the rice also; and now the initiation is complete. Then a gift of a small sum of money together with betel-leaves and arecanuts is made to the *Guru*; and then all together partake of the eatables prepared for the occasion; and the man goes his way.

Thenceforth the boy is put in charge of a village teacher who first teaches him to write correctly on sand spread on the floor all the fifty-one letters of our alphabet, and pronounce them correctly. This might occupy some months. This is preparatory to his being promoted to the stage of writing on cadjans; which process is called *Olayil Kuttal.* After passing through the said preparatory stage the boy begins to write on cadjans instead of on sand as hitherto. After he becomes versed in writing on cadjans, small slokas and other poetical pieces are given to him which he easily commits to memory without understanding their meaning or their significance. When the advanced stages are passed the education is practically complete. But a little before that he is made to acquaint himself with reading our Puranas chiefly the Ramayana.

Elements of arithmetic are also taught by the teacher. Then if the guardians are so minded they place their boys for tuition under the care of some advanced teachers and give them higher instruction in Sanskrit and mathematics; which latter may come even up to the calculation of the position of the planets and the casting of horoscopes. Little girls are also taught elementary music preliminary to their receiving advanced training in it.

The village schools are of the rudest models, being small sheds erected with roofings of cocoanut leaves and pillars and beams of bamboo or cocoanut materials, and a slightly raised floor. Every morning the boys gather there about 7 o'clock when the teacher also attends. He sits down amidst the boys listening to their deafening recitations of things which he has given them to get up by heart; and when a boy tells him that he has finished the work entrusted to him, the teacher asks him to repeat it by heart. If the teacher is satisfied he gives the boy another piece. So runs the process. He thus goes on with the work till about ten in the morning; and then the class is dissolved and the teacher and his boys all depart home to take their meals. About one or two o' clock in the evening these gather again in the school and the same process of instruction is continued. But the reading of the Ramayana or other Puranas is an essential feature of this evening instruction. Till 5 or 5-30 in the evening they go on and then the school closes for the day. But before so closing the boys are made to repeat with one voice some mathematical formulas.

No seats are supplied in the school. But students have

to carry their own small mats with them for seats if they like. The *Ashtami* day which comes round twice every month is invariably a general holiday. On this particular day the imparting of instruction is strictly prohibited. Then again from the *Dwadasi* day up to the *Pratipadam* day (both inclusive) the boys are given a short vacation. Since these days practically come round twice a month, there are two short vacations of five days each for every village school; so that altogether including the *Ashtami* holidays twelve days are holidays every month for all village schools. Of course the Onam, Vishu and other important occasions are necessarily holidays.

Twice a month on the *Dwadasi* day *i.e.*, the beginning of the holidays, the village teacher is remunerated with fees by the boys; which oftentimes vary from one pie to half an anna or so. Many boys right skilfully evade even this paltry payment by absenting themselves on these days. During the Onam and Vishu days the teacher takes care to go round to the houses of the rich amongst his pupils and receives presents of a rupee or below together with two pieces of cloth from the guardians or parents of his pupils. These constitute the main perquisites of his office; and if he be one specially retained by some family he, of course, gets his pay and meals therefrom. During the short vacations allowed to the boys they are usually asked to bring on the re-opening day, as home exercises, a number of cadjans carefully written by them.

The *ferule* or the common birch is freely made use of by the teacher. He is the centre of the admiration and respect and awe of his pupils. His word is law to them; and he is invested with a singular importance in their eyes. His income is extremely meagre; and yet contentment is his lot; and we may well enough say with Oliver Goldsmith,

"A man he *is* to all the country dear,
And passing rich with *few rupees* a year."

Our books are called *Grandhams* and are exclusively made of palm leaves written on with an iron stile called an *Ezhuttani* or *Narayam*. But the introduction of printed books has considerably helped to supplant them. Memory plays the chief role in our village education which mainly consists in the initiation into the three R's. Now village schools after western models are springing up amidst us with marvellous rapidity; and those of the simple indigenous type are gradually disappearing. So much for our village education.

Secondly there is the *village astrologer* called the *kanisan* whose services are of hourly utility in all our social concerns. He has to find out lucky and unlucky days and moments for the commencement of all important business, to note the exact moment of a child's birth for the purpose of casting its horoscope afterwards. He has to bring to leading families on the Onam and Vishu occasions a cadjan chit predicting the consequences arising to the country at large on account of those festivals falling on the particular days of the year; to find out proper physicians for the treatment of diseases;

and to find out proper days and moments for starting on journeys and for many other things such as marriage, tonsure, sowing seeds at seed-time etc. His profession is now largely encroached upon by astrologers from other castes as well. But he is the recognized claimant for the purposes enumerated.

The next claimant is the *village carpenter*, who has to do everything connected with our architecture; such as fixing poles or wickets at the exact spot where buildings are to be erected and to clear newly-erected buildings of all devils and demons that may be haunting them. This he does by means of poojas performed after the completion of the buildings. But people have now begun to break through the village traditions and to entrust architectural work to competent hands when the village carpenter is found incompetent for the same.

The *village goldsmith* has to make ornaments of gold and silver to be put on by our infants for their rice-giving ceremonies and thereafter.

The village *magician or conjurer* goes by different names in different places, such an *Panans Malayans &c.* His work consists in casting out petty devils from the bodies of persons (chiefly children) possessed and to write charms for them to wear; to remove the pernicious effects of evil eye and so on.

The *village washerman* has to do all the washing work in his village. He is required to furnish new-washed clothes for use on festive occasions in temples.

The *village barber* has likewise his place in our village economy. He has to shave children for the first time in their lives; and to shave males on the day they begin to take part in the sacrificial offerings to the departed souls in our families; and also on the last day of our Deeksha ceremonies on the forty-first day or at the end of the first year. All these are attended with solemn ceremonials. Barbers from stranger villages are not on any account to poach upon his work. The barber women are in some parts our village midwives and accouchers whose services are in requisition during childbirth. There are some experts amongst them who can skilfully manage midwifery. In other places the *Velans or Malayans etc.*, (certain sects of low caste p eople) are the professional class for such work.

Then there are the village *Mannans* or *Vannans* who come in for their share of our village duties. Their services are in requisition amongst us during our *Thirandukallianam* ceremonies (*Vide Chapter* on "the Nair Tarawad") when they have to bring for the girls' use their *mattu* or sacred dress. Then on occasions of death-pollution, they have a similar duty to perform. Amongst us on the fourth or rarely on the third day after menses, our women have to use during their bath clothes supplied by these *Mannan* females. Failure to purify their persons with them on the part of our women will be sufficient for outcasting them. The same duty these *Mannan* females have to perform during the confinement period of our females. All the dirty clothes and bed sheets used during such periods, these *Mannan* females have to wash and bring punctually and regularly.

These all are called *Desa avakasikal* or *Jemmis* or *Cheru Jenmakkar i.e.*, birthright-holders. Mr. Logan speaks of these in his Manual of Malabar as follows:—"This organisation is to a certain extent preserved and most probably the *Kanisan's* profession will survive all other relics of the Hindu constitution as his services are still considered of essential importance in all matters of every-day life."

VILLAGE PASTIMES.

Of our dramatic performances, the *Kathakali* and *Krishnattam* are the two foremost ones. A detailed description of these will be found in the chapter on the "Malabar Drama."

Patthavom Parayal is an allied institution. Principally on important festive occasions, inside the temple-walls and outside the buildings and in front of the god some Brahmin well versed in Puranic lore dresses himself up in clothes and a turban, smears his body with ashes and sandal and begins to pace along there repeating in a solemn and dignified fashion some interesting masterpieces from the Sanskrit literature and explain their meaning to the assembled spectators.

The *Koottu* or more properly *Chakkiar Koottu* is a similar institution dating from immemorial times. The *Chakkiars* are a peculiar sect of people. They are said to be the offspring of Brahmin parents begotten as the result of intercourse during menses. Hence they are a socially fallen caste.

On important *utsavam* and other occasions the *koottu* is performed inside buildings attached to temples and specially set apart for the purpose. The actor dresses up in a quaint style with brumagem bracelets on the forearms and the feet. Around his waist he ties a peculiar cloth with a ridiculous profusion of folds all round and reaching barely up to the knee. He wears a head-dress also; and with ashes and sandal smeared all over the body comes in to perform his *koottu*. Chakkiar women are known as *Nangiars*, one of whom is always present by the side of the Chakkiar when engaged in his performance. A tom-tom is beaten by one called *Nambiar* in the interval between the recitation of slokas and the explanation of their meanings. The *koottu* consists in the recitation by the *Chakkiar* of certain Puranic slokas and in his comments on them; which he does in very funny and pointed ways.

The *Chakkiars* are formidable critics of men and things. They always possess the requisite cleverness to apply the context of a recited sloka in an extremely amusing fashion to particular persons amongst the assembled spectators and making the whole company of them enjoy a hearty laugh over it. The received etiquette is that no one is to take offence at jokes cracked by *Chakkiars* nor even laugh loudly at them; any infraction of this etiquette will sufficiently justify their suddenly stopping the performance. They are of course remunerated by the temple authorities.

Mohaniyattam is an institution much akin to the *Dasy-*

attam of the east coast. A leader obtains the services of two or three young girls of low birth and trains them in the obscene technicalities of the profession. This leader is called the *Nettuvan*. He takes these girls from house to house and gets a paltry allowance for each day's performance, and thus they make a living. It is performed usually at nights, when the girls are robed in the finest attire and the dance begins led, of course, by the *Nettuvan*. All sorts of obscene practices are resorted to during the process. This institution is an extremely abominable one. The females who are thus rented out are looked upon in civilized circles with the utmost contempt; and it may be said that they exist as a separate isolated class with little or no community of social interest with other classes. It is some satisfaction to find that the institution is gradually dying a silent and natural death.

The *Tullals* are another class of pastimes amongst us. They may be divided into three distinct varieties such as *Ottan*, *Seetankan* and *Parayan*; of which the two latter are of the most primitive type. But *Ottan* is a little more advanced one in which the actor assumes the form of one of our dramatic actors. Usually only one of these will be acting at a time. The *Tullals* are a singular variety of poetic composition with a peculiar kind of metre, rhyme and rhythm. The actor repeats these stanza by stanza and illustrates the same with significant and suitable gestures. Drums are beaten during the process.

Cheruppinutoli is a pastime gradually dying out too. It is almost indigenous to the south. Two trained bullocks, belonging to different persons are yoked to the same plough; and both are driven together by some one from behind with the utmost possible speed within the limits of a small area of rice-field after harvest. After the bullocks have gone two rounds or three the issue is declared in favour of the owner of that bullock which continues to run however slightly in advance of the other without slackening speed or showing signs of fatigue. Then these bullocks are changed and another two are similarly yoked; and the process is continued for sometime.

Rope-dancing or acrobatic performances constitute another of these enjoyments.

Football-matches, *Attakkalam* and *Kayyankali* and dancing by females called *Kayyukottikali* have all been already described in the chapter on "The Onam Festival." *Whist, cards and dice* are quite common enough particularly during festive seasons.

Cock-fighting is an interesting pastime. Cocks are specially reared and trained to take part in fights. The Uzhinjal swinging has been already described in the chapter on "Tiruvatira Festival."

THE MONTH OF KARKATAKAM.

This is an important month in Malabar though the nature of agriculture here and the constant failure of our monsoons and other causes of a like nature render the period one of poverty, distress and disease. It is one of cleanliness and piety all around. On the first day of the month what is called *Veliyum panalum kuttal* is observed. Clods of earth with growing grass and plants on are deposited one on each corner of the thatching of the house. Members of families bathe early in the mornings, wear the caste marks, dress neatly and begin to read the Puranas, mainly the Ramayana. This of course is continued up to the close of the month. The whole work is read at least once in the month; but there are some who finish it many times during the period. But reading the sacred Puranas, however little, is of essential religious importance at this season of the year.

After the bath is over what is called *Sreebhagavathikku Vekkal* comes on every day in the morning. This consists in placing in a secluded corner of the house, a lighted lamp in front of a small wooden plank on which are also arranged some flowers, a casket of ashes, a grandha or old book made of palmyra leaves, and a new-washed cloth and two measures of rice.

In the night-time on some day in the month after the inmates have all gone to sleep, some *Panars* (a degraded class of people) dress themselves in a peculiar style and come to the gates of all houses singing certain ballads; which wakes up the inmates from slumber. Its significance appears to be to cast out devils from these houses. This institution is called *Thukil Unarttal.*

Then again, during the month we have the ceremonies called *Nara* and *Puttari*. This period is one of our harvest seasons. Before the harvest is over and when the ears of corn are still full ripe, the *Nara* ceremony is performed. Stalks of certain plants and creepers together with some ears of paddy are all kept inside a basket at the gate-house. Now certain figures circular, horizontal and perpendicular are drawn in the outer and inner courtyards of the house and on the floor of the house in prominent places. Then some one who has bathed early takes the basket in hand and repeatedly muttering in an audible tone *Nara Nara*, *Illam Nara*, *Pattayom*, *Nara*, *Vatti Nara*. *Kotta Nara &c.* keeps the same in the inner yard where some poojahs are performed before they are taken out. Then some raw rice already prepared from that particular years, paddy is cooked and sweetened with sugar ; and all the inmates then partake of the preparation. The consumption of new rice (*i.e.*, that particular year's rice) is strictly prohibited before going through this ceremony. For both *Nara* and *Puttari* auspicious moments have to be selected. Both these may be performed on one and the same day or they may be on different days according to the turning up of the auspicious day and convenience of the people. Considerable importance is also attached to the auspicious nature or otherwise of the first guest or animal or thing that finds its way to the house immediately after the *Nara* ceremony ; and the prosperous career of the family for the whole of the ensuing year depends upon the nature of the first-comer.

Then again, on the last day of the month the ceremony called *Jeshtayekalayal* has to be performed. About 6 in the evening a broken earthen pot or a torn sieve is taken and inside it are gathered some old pieces of broomsticks, bits of human hair and nails and some sweepings and other filthy substances and some arrowroot plants. Some one then takes this along with a lighted torch and carries it to every nook and corner of the house. This is then handed over outside to some menial servant to be carried away to some distant three-cornered road or pathway to be thrown off there. On his way thither the servant is subjected to all kinds of vile abuse. This drives off the *Jeshta* or unclean diety from the house making it wholly pure and clean.

Nothing more appears necessary to be said on the subject. Of course there are more things of lesser importance and interest that I may, with propriety, dwell upon in this connection. But in an attempt of this nature it is hardly necessary or possible to enter into such minute details.

CHAPTER XV.

SOME PHASES OF RELIGIOUS LIFE.

Like all other parts of India, Malabar is a deeply religious country. Every one here believes more or less firmly in the existence of an Overruling Providence, who sways the universe, rewards the just and the virtuous, and metes out condign punishment to the guilty and the sinful. This Being, who is the Creator and Preserver of the world, is seated on high in the celestial regions, from whence He exerts His divine influence on all created things. He is without form, or if He has any form at all, it is unseen of men because of the dazzling brilliance of the light which emanates from Him in all directions. Usually He is regarded as the Unseen, the Unknown and the Unknowable. He is placed on a throne of resplendent glory, attended by angels and demigods, who are at His immediate beck and call. He is Omnipresent, Omnipotent, and Omniscient, and takes care of the tiniest of His creations as well as the largest. Plants, animals and all created objects are the creatures of His will. Worlds can be annihilated or called into existence by means of His all-powerful breath. He understands the deeds and motives of every one of His creatures. A recording angel takes account of all our actions, which find reward or punishment at the close of our earthly life. Such is the power of God as He exists in the popular imagination. The heavenly regions, where He is seated, are regions of eternal plenty, bliss, prosperity and joy to which admission is guranteed only to the righteous.

In marked contrast with these regions is the hell of the popular imagination. It is a place of a perpetual torment agony, sorrow and affliction. By some, it is looked upon as a huge burning lake full of an abominable fluid, containing multitudinous varieties of worms and other equally disgusting forms of animal life. Its horrors are indescribable. It is the destined abode of sinners, who according to the heinousness of their sins are condemned to live there for varying intervals of time. The animals which live there ceaselessly molest the guilty. Thus the horrors are rendered all the more intense and insufferable. Some people regard the hellish regions as being situated below the earth; while others locate them somewhere up in the heavens. But in either case they are directly within the sight and control of the Almighty God.

The people of Malabar are invariably believers in a future life of some sort. A man lying at the point of death is supposed to be haunted by spirits who await the drawing of his last breath. If he be a man, who has led a life unspotted from the world, death to him is altogether a pleasing incident. He will be carried into the upper regions by bright-looking beings in cars profusely decorated and lighted up with glowing lamps and scented with an abundance of perfumery. In his journey up, in this Elysian conveyance, he will be accompanied by attendants ready even to lay down their lives at his call. He will be received in the heavenly regions by guards who will take him to his proper place there. There he will live in everlasting bliss and comfort. Some people, however hold that he will in certain cases assume his human shape a second time and be born again on the earth. But if he is to remain in heaven, his state of bliss and joy will know no bounds. He will live in the presence of God and will receive every possible attention from God's servants. He will hold communion with his departed friends and relatives who have become the inhabitants of those regions. This conception of immortality and of intercourse hereafter with dead friends and relatives is very similar to the view of the future life taken by Tennyson in his *In memoriam.* Finally, permanent assimilation with God, according to some advanced thinkers brings a man's human existence to a close.

But the state of a man who has lived a sinful life is a terrible contrast to that described above. Even on his death bed huge monstrous looking figures surround him at all times and especially towards the closing moments of his earthly career. These make mouths at him, threaten him, terrify him, informing him that the horrors to which he is being subjected are but the mild precursors of those which await him in the nether regions. These beings are visible to him alone, none of those who stand by being able to see these terrible monsters. According to the pre-destined period of his life, the man may have to exist in this wretched state for days and days together. After his death, he is taken care of by a monster called Kalan. This monster, is furnished with a long rope, and an iron pestle; and with the aid of his grisly-looking attendants he strings up the dead man on his pestle and carries him off into the upper regions. There he is taken before God, when the celestial recorder, called Chitraguptan, brings forth his books and reads out a full and correct account of all the man's actions. His sins are to be expiated by horrible punishments inflicted then and there, followed by similar and more lasting ones to be undergone later. A large copper vessel is brought and placed over a burning oven. When the fire burns intensely underneath, so that the vessel is practically white hot, it is half filled with sand. When the sand begins to burn, the sinner is placed in the vessel and by means of a large rod with a spread out tip, he is moved to and fro along with the burning sand. He dies again, is forthwith restored to life, and the process is continued time after time. Afterwards he is taken out and sent to the hellish regions to suffer the pains and torments, incidental to life there. Some believe that he is kept there for ever. But according to others when by the continued misery of his existence in hell, he has sufficiently well atoned for his past sins, he is released in order to be born back again into this world and so on *ad infinitum.* It ought to be stated that the conveyance in which men are taken to the upper regions to stand their trial before God, threatens every moment to collapse and let them fall. According to some, they are compelled to ascend into the upper regions on a rope-ladder of slender construction which also every now and then threatens to give way under the weight of its human passengers. Their destruction or escape in either of these cases depends upon the good or evil nature of their worldly actions. An adulterer is punished in a peculiar manner after death. He is conveyed to the judgment seat of God and is there compelled to embrace a metal image which is heated almost to whiteness. When the fierceness of the heat has consumed his body, he is again brought back to life and subjected to the same form of punishment. The process is repeated as often as has been guilty of adulterous conduct before his death.

Traditions of a ridiculous nature have clustered round this notion of men being carried up by Kalan on his iron pestle. There is a fable which I believe is current in various parts of Malabar according to which a man whose course of worldly existence was not completely overrun, was carried up by this monster by mistake. When he arrived at the seat of God, the mistake was found out and the man was dropped down again to the earth to complete his term of life. As his funeral had not been begun in the meanwhile his body still remained in his house and the people who stood near it, little suspecting that he was not dead, were extremely surprised to find him breathing again. The next day they were still more astonished to find marks of violence on his body, which appeared to be marks left by the process of tying him up on the pestle the previous day. Moreover, these inferences were corroborated when the man himself related to those present the circumstances of his death and of his being tied up, carried above, and dropped down again.

Whatever may be the heinousness of a man's sins, he can be saved in various ways from eternal torment and ranked in point of merit with the most virtuous. Paying money, cloths and other objects to the twice-born Brahmins, redeems a man from the consequences of his sins. Such gifts may be made during a man's life-time even up to the time of his death.

Feeding Brahmins is also productive of similar results. A man who has periodically paid money to Brahmins chiefly of the Nambudri class is said to be "saved." Every family regularly makes a point of observing feasts and feeding Brahmins and paying them money and receiving their blessings. There are also other expedients resorted to during a man's life-time, whereby such results can be more or less effectually attained. Certain days, such as Ekadasi, are ordained as fasting days. Such fastings require only abstinence from rice meals, spirituous liquors and animal food and from the enjoyment of worldly pleasures and if religiously continued up to the close of life will secure for a man an easy and pleasant death, and become stepping stones to the regions of heaven, where a life of bliss and joy will be his portion. Offerings to gods residing in temples are also of great efficacy. Pilgrimages undertaken to any of the great centres of popular worship such as Benares, Rameswaram and Gaya are also equally efficacious. Bathing in the Ganges or the Kaveri or some other sacred river as also in sanctified waters of Rameswaram will wash away all a man's sins. Reading any of the sacred *Puranas*, the *Mahabaratha* the *Ramayana* or the *Bhagavatha* is another equally meritorious method of obtaining absolution from past sins. Hindu prayers are mostly but the continuous mention of the names of the chief members of the Divine Trinity. The repetition of the names of any of Vishnu's various incarnations, such as, Rama and Krishna forms an equally effectual prayer. The popular idea is that a man performs twenty-one thousand acts of respiration in a day ; and whoever prays in the manner indicated these twenty-one thousand times, that is whoever mentions the name of any of these gods twenty-one thousand times a day is said to be absolved completely from that day's sins. Smearing the body, especially the forehead and the breast and the arms with ashes prepared from cow-dung is another way of cleansing the body and the soul. Sandal-juice preparation forms a desirable accessory to cow-dung ashes. In these various ways a man can be purified from a sinful life and admitted to heaven's eternal bliss. Besides obtaining the guarantee of a life in heaven, if he is to be born again into this world he will become a twice-born Brahmin.

When a man is on his death-bed, Brahmins are invited to his house and offerings of money are given to them together with clothes, some betel-leaves and nuts. The Brahmins accept these things and with uplifted hands invoke the aid of God and bless the man. This purifies him from his past sinful life. Sometimes the offering consists of cows, which form a still higher and more acceptable kind of gift. Then also offerings of *Puja* are made to various gods through the medium of Brahmin priests to save a man from a life in the infernal regions. Sweet drinks are given to weary and thirsty travellers, whose blessings carry very happy results. *Rice Kunji* is given to the class of people called *Nayadis*. These things are all done when a men is on his death bed; and they have the effect of purifying the man and obtaining for him entrance into the heaven.

Some people hold that a man's sins are all to be expiated in this world and that after death he immediately proceeds to the next birth. So also in the case of rewards. A sinner is supposed to be purified from his sins by means of the miseries and calamities to which he is subjected up till the last moment of his life, such miseries and calamities being in themselves sufficient atonement for all his sins; and the happiness and joy that fall to the lot of a good man are likewise regarded as the necessary rewards for his good and virtuous life. According to this belief, men reap the consequences of their acts in this world and in this world alone and death is but the opening out of another life in this world or as some others believe in a still happier world and not an absolute and entire cessation of life altogether. This is very much akin to the sentiment expressed by Mrs. Barbauld in the lines.

> " Say not 'good night"—but in some brighter clime,
> Bid me 'good morning.'

Such are some of the popular ideas about rewards and punishments both in this life and in the life that is to come. In all of them, there is present the belief in a future life of some sort; and they distinctly exclude conceptions of a materialistic kind which deny a divine Providence and human responsibility.

The various acts which, in Malabar, are regarded as sinful may now be mentioned. Falsehood, forgery, perjury, suicide, and homicide of every description are of course prominent among these. Speaking ill of gods and Brahmins is a blasphemous sin. Polluting any shrine, eating at times of pollution, and before bathing and false swearing are likewise sinful. So also are the taking of rice preparations on prohibited days and at prohibited moments, and neglect to bathe and cleanse the body every day. "Laying irreverant hands upon the dear inheritance of our forefathers," such as old institutions and want of deference to seniors and elders, and above all to teachers and Brahmins, are also placed in the category of sins. Talking slightingly of the sun or the moon and injuring any of the sacred animals such as kites, cows, bulls, lizards, serpents, scorpions and certain kinds of fishes, specially bred in tanks attached to certain temples which are invested with varying degrees of sanctity are also regarded as sins.

The religious creed of the Malayalee tallies exactly with the idea expressed so beautifully by Wordsworth in the well-known stanza:—

"Our birth is but a sleep and a forgetting:
The soul that rises with us, our life's star
Hath had elsewhere its setting,
And cometh from afar.
Not in entire forgetfulness,
And not in utter nakedness,
But trailing clouds of glory do we come
From God, who is our home.
Heaven lies about us in our *infancy* ;
Shades of the prison-house begin to close
Upon the growing *boy*,
But he beholds the light, and whence its flows,
He sees it in his joy ;
The *youth* who daily farther from the east
Must travel, still is nature's priest
And by the vision splendid
Is on his way attended.
At length the *man* perceives it die away,
And fade into the light of common day."

Death is regarded not as an entire cessation of life here, but as the beginning of another life. "The soul never dies. It passes from body to body in successive births." This represents the universal creed of the people. The child is conceived in its mother's womb and after a certain time is born. At its birth it finds itself in a world which is altogether strange to it. It is completely enveloped by the glories of its past life and knows absolutely nothing about the circumstances and surroundings of the world. It grows up little by little; and as it grows, it grows in knowledge and experience. It begins to take an interest in the persons and objects around it, and the alternation of laughing and weeping shows that it is also beginning to know something of the joy and sorrow of human life.

The common country folk attribute the alternations of joy and sorrow manifested in the face of a child to a peculiar cause. They believe that there is a particular species of devils, who are in constant attendance upon children. At times these creatures take delight in annoying the little ones. They tell them that their fathers or their mothers have died. This, of course, makes them weep. On the other hand, when the devils tell the children that their parents have been brought back to life, the little ones are intensely pleased. Thus it is the mischievous doings of these devils that give birth to the various manifestations of feeling noticed in the faces of children.

As the child grows up, the thoughts of its past life

vanish and are supplanted by those of this life, so that by the time it reaches the age of manhood, remembrance of its past entirely fades away yielding place to the concerns and incidents of this life. The eating of salt, it is said, gradually brings this about. Hence until children reach a certain age the practice is invariably insisted upon of not giving them salt along with their food.

There are familiar traditions which have gathered round the last death-struggles of some men. It is said that those who are professed *mantravadis* or magicians are sometimes subjected to these death-pangs. The particular demons whom these magicians, by the power of their spells, have conquered and held in subjection enter into fierce struggles with the celestial carrier when he takes them away into the upper regions. This the demons do with the object of saving the lives of their masters. Sometimes the contest rages long; but in no case does it eventuate in the triumph of the devil and the defeat of the carrier.

When after death the spirit or the soul of the man departs the body is left behind; and when it is disposed of it becomes part and parcel of the earth-clod, whence it was taken for purposes of creation. The departed soul continues to haunt the vicinity of the house of the deceased. One theory is, that it goes upwards, and is taken to the presence of God in the manner described above. Another is that, to the virtuous man is given a birth superior to his past one, such as that of a *Nambudri* Brahmin; while to a vicious man is accorded a troublesome and miserable second birth, such as that of one of the lower animals. Those who hold this theory also believe that since the Brahmin birth is the last link in the long chain of births, a man who proves virtuous again in his Brahmin life is allowed to enjoy for ever the pleasures and comforts of heaven in the presence of God, and is finally absorbed into Him. To those who hold this belief, absorption into the Diety is indeed the last and

> "One far-off divine event
> To which the whole creation moves."

The souls of some persons continue to haunt the vicinity of their houses, looking to the members of the household for sustenance. On the death of a man and after the funeral ceremonies are over, the junior members of his household begin to perform ceremonies in propitiation of the spirit of the departed man. For fifteen days the ceremonies go on; and all this time the death pollution continues. During this period, the members of the household as well as of the whole clan of which it forms a unit, must keep aloof from all social intercourse and dealings with other people. But in North Malabar the pollution period varies much sometimes being twelve days sometimes thirteen &c. On fifteenth day, they have to undergo the purification rites and then and not till then do they get cleansed so as to admit of their moving again in society. On the fifteenth day the ceremonies practically cease; and then such of the members as desire to continue taking part in them are at liberty to do so. Some of the members, however, continue, and on the forty-first day those who are so minded have another chance of leaving off. But the nearest relatives of the deceased continue to perform the ceremonies till the close of the first year. The female members who join in the performance, invariably leave off on the forty-first day; but resume it forty-one days previous to the end of the first year. Thus the males and the females begin and conclude the ceremonies together. During the year, there are particular ceremonies to be performed in addition to the daily ones. For instance at the close of every month, a *masum* ceremony has to be gone through. It lasts for a single day. The ceremony described above as lasting for a whole year goes by the distinctive appellation of *Deeksha*. Any person who is engaged in performing the *Deeksha* ceremony is strictly prohibited from shaving his hair or cutting his nails, from indulging in animal food or intoxicating drinks, from yielding to the temptations of the flesh, from eating anything before bathing when once he has mixed with society and even from breaking his touch with the earth. In short he has to lead a life of complete self-resignation from all mundane concerns. Then at the close of the first year the daily performance of the ceremonies ceases and the performer returns to the ordinary concerns of his life; but every year, on the return of the day of the man's death a ceremony called a *Srarda* has to be performed. Since our *years* correspond to the *days* of the spiritual world our annual

Srarda ceremonies, though performed only once a year, become daily offerings to the departed. In ways such as these, departed spirits are propitiated. The strict observance of these ceremonies protects the family from all calamities; while neglect of them is visited with serious consequences. Thus what is called Moksham is obtained for the person.

Another method by which a like boon is obtained for him is interesting. After the disposal of the body, the bones are collected and placed in new and unused earthen pots and deposited inside the earth near the southern side of the house. Sometime after, these are taken to one of the principal centres of worship and after due ceremonies have been performed, they are thrown into the waters of some sacred river near the shrine.

Evil spirits of various descriptions are supposed to haunt the neighbourhoods of burial and cremation grounds and hence people have a peculiar dread of approaching these places at night. The *ignis fatuus* of marshy places has been converted by the popular imagination into demons who are looked upon as the possessors of these spots.

A woman dying during pregnancy or after delivery and before the pollution period is completed, is supposed to have a wandering state of existence after death. Her spirit is polluted and is incapable of purification in the ordinary way. Hence it cannot gain entrance either into heaven or into hell, her polluted condition being inconsistent with the sanctity of those worlds. Therefore in order that it may be purified and rendered capable of re-birth it must be subjected to a process of cleansing by means of *mantrams* and *pujas* and other incidental rites at the hands of the Brahmin priests. If it is left unpurified by means of proper offerings, the consequences to the family may be of the most dreadful and disastrous kind. It is said to wander about the four corners of the house, uttering a shrill hideous cry which forebodes a calamitous future for the family. The cry is said to resemble the cry of women in child-birth.

I have, in the opening pages of this paper described some of the higher phases of our religious life in Malabar. But the belief in the existence of a Supreme Power guiding the course of the world is sadly corrupted by the prevalence of notions verging on the worst forms of superstition. The Almighty God presides over everything created and uncreated. Under Him, however, countless gods and goddesses are conceived to exist and are given local habitations in wooden and stone images. Krishna, the chief incarnation of Vishnu, is a god zealously worshipped by the people. So also Vishnu himself and Siva. The goddess *Kali* presides over all infectious diseases, such as cholera and small-pox. She has a number of daughters located in different parts of the country with delegated powers which are exercised within certain specified areas, subject to the authority of Kali herself. When small-pox and cholera are epidemic in any locality, these goddesses meet together at the people's request and after proper propitiatory ceremonies have been performed they together drive the devils and free the country from their merciless devastations. When a man is attacked with small-pox, the goddess of his locality is invited by special offerings to his house. She manifests herself by leaping and shoutings in the body of her human representative, who, with the sword he holds in his hand and the red cloth that he wears round his waist, drives away small-pox demons and saves the patient from death. Year after year these goddesses visit the houses situated in their respective jurisdictions.

One important annual event connected with the worship of *Kali* is the *Cock-festival* at Cranganore, the abode of this goddess. (*Vide* Chapter on Cock-Festival.)

There are other dieties who are located in particular parts of the country and to whom definite powers are assigned. Among such are Bharadevatha, Ganapati, Ayyappan, Vavar, Karal, Vettekkaran and others. They are invoked in special emergencies when they render their assistance to those who so invoke them. One peculiar god who is very zealously worshipped is Subramanian whose temple is situated on the Palni Hills. Incredible miracles are often ascribed to him. He is said to possess the power of restoring to life, animals which after having been killed, cut up and cooked, have been taken to his shrine as offerings by pilgrims and, of preserving from putrefaction milk which has been kept for months and similarly carried up to the hills. Other miracles also are attributed to him. Ayyappan is believed to protect people from the attacks of wild beasts. In the extreme south of the country, there is a curious god called Chathan who is an evil deity capable only of working mischief. He lends his aid to any one who prays for it with proper offerings. The person against whom his aid is invoked is put to every kind of annoyance, from which he can rid himself only by means of a propitiatory ceremony. In some parts, a certain cattle god called Mundian is worshipped who is also invested with detective powers in petty cases of theft. All these and others, which cannot even be enumerated testify to the great hold which idolatry has on the people of Malabar.

There are also nymphs, nereids and other beings who are supposed to possess powers of mischief-working and in consequence are regarded by the people with reverence and fear. These attack people while passing their abodes and bring on temporary attacks of disease. There exist yet two other classes of beings called Yakshies and Gandharvas. The former are a kind of goddesses of gigantic proportions, with large teeth, flashing fiery eyes, hair clotted and flying about, and dark bodily colour. They as well as the Gandharvas live on palm-trees and attack men and women indiscriminately. When once a person is possessed with them, it is impossible to get rid of them except by very powerful incantations; and in most cases attempts at casting them out prove altogether fruitless. Sometimes they consent of ther own accord to retire from human bodies and leave them unmolested. These and similar deities are not worshipped by means of images.

A few words about sorcery and witchcraft or mantravadams will not be wholly out of place here. These mantravadams are usually divided into two categories, namely, the good and the evil. It is supposed that the good ones were given in exclusive monopoly to one particular Brahmin family and the evil ones to another, both in south Malabar, and that they were afterwards surreptitiously copied by people, not all Brahmins. Certain deities are invoked and overpowered by means of mantrams, and these are ready to stand by the Mantravadis, or magicians, in times of need. When epilepsy and other nervous diseases which are attributed to the mischievous influences of spirits occur in any family the member possessed is effectually cured by the magic of some skilled exorcist. The devil can be compelled to state his name and history through the mouth of the patient. Then according to his power, he is either compelled to leave the patient's body for good or he is properly propitiated and in consequence consents to depart from it promising not to molest it again. These magicians even possess the power of taking away human lives through the instrumentality of *Mantrams*. Anything that they require can be supplied to them from any distance by these evil spirits.

Religious worship in all it prestine simplicity still obtains in a diversity of forms in Malabar. There are, for instance, forms of ancestor-worship, animal-worship, tree-worship serpent-worship, and demon-worship, still religiously followed. Reference has already been made to ancestor-worship in connection with the death-pollution ceremony. Deceased ancestors are practically deified and offerings are made to them for their satisfaction and propitiation, neglect of such duties being visited with serious misfortunes to their families. Annual ceremonies are also performed to them. As regards animal-worship, people have a peculiar veneration for certain beasts, such as the ox, the cow, the bull, the lizard, and the elephant; for certain birds, such as the kite and the pea-cock, all of which are surrounded with a tinge of religious sanctity. The cow and the Brahmin are placed on an equal footing in point of holiness, and are looked upon as the most sacred of God's creatures. Hence the killing, of either of these, is the most heinous sin that a man can be guilty of. The lizard is a prophet of future events and is also regarded as sacred by the people. The kite is the vehicle of Krishna and hence a very sacred creature like the ox which is of the vehicle of Siva. There are other animals considered more or less sacred, but I cannot say more on this subject at present. Tree-worship has also been developed into a kind of religious ordinance. The banyan-tree is held in great veneration as also the *Kuvalam*. The plant called *Tulasi* is equally holy. The *Kuvalam* tree is a tree peculiarly sacred to Siva; and hence people make a point preserving it by means of laterite work to strengthen the roots. In the evening they place lighted torches or lamps near it and children and even grown up men go and worship it in the belief that this will have much the same effect as worshipping in a temple dedicated to Siva. Banyan-trees are also kept in a similar state of preservation. The Kuvalam leaves are appropriate objects of worship in temples, especially in Sivite temples. As regards devil-worship many spirits such as Kurin-kutty, Kutti-Chathan, and a number of other wandering demons, are given local abodes in images and are duly worshipped and oftentimes conquered; so that in cases of emergency, their services in the protection of human lives are exacted. These beings have no proper place assigned to them in the Hindu creed; but are native to Malabar, where they have obtained a firm hold upon the popular imagination. For serpent-worship *Vide* Chapter on "Serpent-Worship."

The art of prognosticating the future has developed into a science in Malabar and is studied with scrupulous attention by such as seek, to earn a living by means of it. There are varieties of ways in which the future can be disclosed, whether of individuals or of the country at large. Foremost among these is the science of Astrology. As in the case of all who profess the Hindu faith, this science is blindly believed in by the people of Malabar, and its tenets and formulas are closely followed and religiously acted on by them. There are other but less accurate methods of prognostication of which chiromancy forms one. There are experts who have studied the art and profess to be able to reveal any one's future. But it is chiefly the *Kuravars*, a wandering class of people, who are the exponents of this art. These *Kuravars* are said to be the descendants of Gypsies, who found their way into Malabar at some remote epoch of its history. Another method of foretelling the future is by opening at random any one of the great *Puranas* and counting out the first seven lines on the right hand page and the first seven letters in the eighth line on the same page and reading the rest beginning with the eighth letter in the eighth line. From the nature of what is read, the future is foretold. But before the process is begun, the man on whose behalf it is to be undertaken, must shut his eyes and offer a prayer to God requesting him to maintain the accuracy and correctness of the art. This method is employed only when the future of a particular object is to be ascertained. It cannot be easily made use of, in foretelling the whole of a man's future. As observed before, the lizard is a prophet of future events. Experts understand the significance of the lizard's cry. If a lizard happens to make any noise in the midst of an important conversation regarding the future, these experts can foretell in various ways what is about to happen. As for example from the particular mode in which the cry was produced and reached them; from the quarters from which the cry emanated; from the particular movements of the animal, and so on. Omens are also prophetic in certain cases. When a man starts on an important errand, his success or failure will depend upon the peculiar nature, auspicious or otherwise of the object he chances to see immediately after crossing his gateway. The noise produced by owls is also possessed of a like power. If an owl makes a noise from the southern side of a house, then a birth is to be anticipated in the family; but if the noise comes from the north, a death is likely to occur. The howling of dogs, whether singly or in packs, at unseasonable periods of the day and through mere wantonness, foreshadows the approach of *Kalan*, the celestial carrier. Then again, the loud cries of certain depressed races of the country, *viz.*, the Nayadis are prophetic. If any member of a household is dangerously ill, it is customary to institute for some days the gift of kunjy-water to these poor specimens of humanity. They drink the water with great alacrity; and if the ordinary taste of the kunjy turns into that of dead body, the patient will die. If not he will recover. These various methods of prying into the secrets of the future have become part and parcel of the popular religion; and the accuracy and correctness of the various predictions are deemed to depend upon the divine influences underlying them.

The people of Malabar are with few exceptions fatalists. They hold strongly that all their future has been definitely worked out and ordained for them at the moment of their births; that whatever happens to them is only what has been pre-arranged by God before He created them; and that nothing else can possibly befall them. The future destinies of mankind are written upon their heads in characters that no ordinary mortals can decipher and understand. The horizontal and transverse sutures of the skull are popularly identified with the hieroglyphics in which the future of mankind is inscribed. The common saying is: "whatever is written upon our heads will and must come to pass. It is not for mortals to avert the stroke of destiny." Not even God, the Almighty, is able to alter the tide of affairs when once it has begun to flow. The only alternative is to calmly submit to those pre-arranged decrees. The future can be revealed to men by means of the science of the horoscopy in which they blindly believe. But there is one class of people, who, though they are believers in predestination, yet think that by prayers duly offered to God, mainly through the medium of Brahmin priests, the evils of an adverse fate can be greatly mitigated.

A more rational article of popular faith which prevails amongst a still larger circle of people is that all the happiness and misery that men are heir to in this life, are the necessary and inevitable consequences of their actions in the previous birth; and that the fruits of all their actions in this life are to be reaped by them only in the life that lies beyond the grave. Thus a man's life here is rendered happy or miserable according as his actions have been just or unjust in the life through which he has already passed.

According to the popular belief a man who commits a murder in this life is to be similarly murdered in the next life by the same victim and in the manner in which he deals with his victim here. In fact the nature of their positions and acts is exactly reversed in the future life. This is extended even to the case of the minutest animal crawling unnoticed on the surface of the earth. For instance, if a man takes away the life of an ant here, that man in the next life will be born an ant, and the ant a man, so as to kill the ant, his former murderer. The absurdity of the notion is patent enough. Victims of unsatisfied desire in this life are destined to pass through a fresh birth so that they may gratify the desires which they are unable to gratify here.

I need hardly say that I am now concerned only with the followers of Hinduism in Malabar. The Hinduism of the Malayalee presents a very strange diversity of features. We have already seen that that some of the highest conceptions of Hindu philosophy and religion exist side by side with the most puerile of religious superstitions. Ultimate absorption into the Supreme Being as the destined goal of human life. the gradual evolution of all created things towards a higher state of perfection, the doctrine of transmigration and the retention of identity these lofty aud sublime conceptions of philosophy and religion have been attained by a society of people amongst whom also prevail religious conceptions characteristic of the most primitive condition of human society.

———:o:———

A GLOSSARY OF TERMS.

—o—

Adigal.—An almost extinct race of quasi-Brahmins in Malabar.

Amshom.—A political sub-division of a Taluk which is a division of a District presided over by a village headman called an *Adhigari.*

Aripravu.—Brown pigeon.

Arna or Arana.—Salamander.

Chakram.—Throwing disk of Vishnu.

Clan.—A number of collateral families amongst the Nairs bound together by community of pollution, but with no property interests except as remote reversioners. Intermarriages strictly prohibited between the members thus blended.

Cranganore.—Mal: Kodungallur, the former residence of Perumals.

Deshom.—A political sub-division of an Amshom.

Fanom.—An old gold coin current during reigns of the Zamorins of Calicut; not legal tender now, but used as weights and preserved as old curiosities. It is equivalent to 4 as. and 4 as. 7p. sometimes. It is met with in two varieties, the old and the new.

Ganapathi.—The Hindu god who is the remover of obstacles ; half man and half elephant.

Grandha.—A book made of palm leaves.

Jenmies.—Landlords.

Kanji.—A drink consisting of boiled rice together with the water in which the rice is boiled.

Kariastan.—Agent.

Karin kannidal.—Casting evil eye.

Kshathriyas.—The second in order of the four great castes of the Hindus.

Konna.—*Cassia fistula.*

Kuridi.—Blind worm.

Kuvalam.—*Aegle marmelos* holy to Siva.

Lanka.—The Modern Ceylon ; strictly the country governed by the wicked giant Ravana of the Ramayana fame.

Manayola or Manjola.—Red arsenic used for painting cheeks.

Nad.—Country.

Olayil Kootal.—Admitting into the cadjan.

Panchagavyam.—A sacred mixture made of the five products of the cow *viz.*, dung, milk, urine, curds, and ghee used for purifying purposes.

Panar—A low caste people.

Pulluvar.— do do

Palanquins and Dollies.—Two dignified kinds of conveyances used by the old feudal chieftains and rarely at present by their lineal representatives.

Panikkar.—A sub-division amongst the Nairs, the representatives of the old gymnasts and fighters.

Rahu.—The huge serpent who is believed to devour the sun and moon during eclipses.

Tulasi.—The Holy bail, *Ocymum Sanctum.*

Tribe.—A larger unit composed of different *clans*; no property interests. Intermarriages allowed between the members of the *different clans*, but not between those of the same *clan.*

Utsavam.—A religious festival in temples.

Vamana.—Youth; the 5th incarnation of Vishnu.

Vali or *Vazhi.*—When added on to *Nad* or *Deshom* means *ruler.*

Vela.—A religious festival connected with the worship of the subordinate duties of the goddess *Kali*, celebrated chiefly by low caste people near those respective temple premises.

—o—

ERRATA.

PAGE.	LINE.	
5	10	For *Aristo* read *Ariosto.*
6	3	For *girgling* read *gurgling.*
11	26	For justification read *in* justification.
40	12	For *Travels* read *Voyage.*
72	15	Add *of* before unreasoning superstition.
79	16	For *Twin* read *Turn.*
124	22	For *his* read *their.*
127	2	For social *fixity* read social *safety.*

OPINIONS ON THE UPANISHADS.

Prof. Max Muller :—. . . . *Faithful translations of the commentaries . . . . . . would be most useful to make the real character both of the Upanishad and of Sankara better known in England.*

Swami Ramakrishnananda :—The rendering is as concise as it is literal and a man with a partial knowledge of Sanskrit who wants to go through Sankara's invaluable commentaries will never find a better help than this tiny and well-got up volume.

Mr. Bal Gunghadhar Tilak of Poona :—*The work appears to be carefully executed* and I have no doubt that your books will prove to be of great use to the public, especially the English-reading class.

The Theosophical Review, London :—The series will be of service not so much for the translation of the text as for that of the commentary. *The get-up of this book is very creditable. Few books are so well turned out in India.*

The Madras Mail :—Sankara's commentaries on the Upanishads *are translated in this book in an accurate and clear style.*

The Theosophist, Madras :—The eminent scholarship of the translator is a sufficient guarantee for the correct rendering of the Sanskrit-Devanagari text which in all cases precedes the English version.

THE INDIAN REVIEW

(PUBLISHED IN THE FIRST WEEK OF EVERY MONTH)

ANNUAL SUBSCRIPTION Rs. 5 (FIVE). (10s.)

SINGLE COPY As. EIGHT + ONE SHILLING.

The Press on The Indian Review.

The Liberty Review.—The signed articles are of the varied character of our English high class monthly magazines.

The Indian Journal of Education.—Keeps well up to the standard of excellence of its first number and reflects the greatest credit on its conductors.

The Oriental List.—It is with great pleasure that we announce the appearance of a new high class magazine in India * * The Indian Review, published at Madras, promises to be an important organ of native opinion.—

The Madras Mail.—The Review well maintains the bright promise of the first number.

The Madras Times.—It is an excellent periodical.

The Educational Review.—The *Indian Review* deserves, what it is no doubt getting, increasing appreciation. * * There is no periodical in India which approaches it for the money. * * It caters for all readers, and should prove a welcome addition to the reading tables of First-grade Colleges. There is no other periodical in India which is run on exactly the same lines.

The Hindu.—We wish the magazine the success it so well deserves. * * There can be no doubt that enterprises of this sort will mark the beginning of a new era of periodical literature in this country, affording as they do, not only interesting reading to the public, but also scope for the exercise of literary talent among English-educated Indians.

Power and Guardian :—We are sure, if the public rightly appreciate the *Review*, as they should, the future of the magazine is bright and the career long.